'Man, Yo
A Jamaican C

C000293080

'Man, you've mixed' was a common expression among some Jamaicans during the 1940s and 1950s when commenting on how a fellow Jamaican had mixed in with a wide range of different people. It took on a particular significance when used at a time during which there was little mixing between black and white people.

A friend, whom I had not seen for several years, called to see me at my flat. There he was confronted by a variety of people of different races and skin colours all enjoying a party together. In greeting, he shook my hand and remarked: 'Man, you've mixed'.

'Man, You've Mixed': A Jamaican Comes to Britain

Eric Ferron

Whiting and Birch Ltd
MCMXCV

© Eric Ferron, 1995

Published by Whiting & Birch Ltd,
PO Box 872, , London SE23 3HL, England.
USA: Paul & Co, Publishers' Consortium Inc,
PO Box 442, Concord, MA 01742.

British Library Cataloguing in Publication Data.
A CIP catalogue record is available from the British Library

ISBN 1 871177 97 9 (limp)
Printed in England by Bourne Press Limited, Bournemouth.

Contents

Thanks and Dedication

I wish to thank Elizabeth Barnes who has been my main supporter over many years during the writing of my book. I would also like to say thank you to my many friends, black and white, who have stood by me and supported me through many difficulties.

I dedicate this book to my wife Birgitta, my daughters Anna and Maria for their support and love, and the strength I have gained through having them as my family.

Introduction

This book has been written as my autobiography. It recalls my early days in England, from teenage to adulthood. It describes my expectations while coming over, and my dreams about England and my hopes of returning to Jamaica in triumph to build my life anew. It recalls my days in camp, the period of consolidation, learning to behave 'as expected'. To learn to be liked and 'to do the right thing'. It describes my journeys across England, from London to Wales. The angry times, and the hostility I received in pubs in London, Swansea and Somerset, fighting rejection. It recalls how I learned that I was not wanted. It also describes my learning years, how I learned 'how to be' and 'how not to be', the early post-war years and my exposure to society, not as a serviceman but as a black civilian. It describes my first visit to London with Ben, and how I realised that the reality outside camp life was very painful. How I met Ben's family, my disillusionment as well as my hope. It describes many doorstep discussions whilst seeking somewhere to live. How I recalled my childhood when I felt desperate and in need of a glimmer of hope and joy. It describes what I believe to be the Jamaican personality within myself, how I see myself as a Jamaican and how my beliefs were formed. I could compromise, but I could not compromise my pride. I describe also how I have formulated my ideas.

I put this book together because I hope that young people who feel there is no hope may read it and that it will convey to them a strength that will enable them to withstand their difficulties and the things that they are experiencing. That it may help them to realise the value of parents.

I hope the book will also be read by adults who will see how pain can be put to constructive uses. I feel that my journey has accomplished a great deal and that I am learning to assess its results and move further forward in pursuit of my objectives even though as an individual I can only make a small contribution.

Eric Ferron

One

Coming Over

Early one morning in 1944, after nearly two months in the RAF camp in Jamaica, we were awakened and taken by lorries and trucks to Kingston Harbour where a big ship, the SS *Cuba*, was waiting. We were not told we were going to England, but then we always knew we would go.

All through my boyhood I was constantly hoping the time would come. We all did. We had heard about Queen Victoria, about Rodney and Nelson, all the great English sailors and soldiers. Buckingham Palace. Windsor Castle. We had seen pictures of these great buildings and of places in all the great countries of Europe.

I had joined up because I had wanted to get away, do something new, something different. I did not tell my parents I had applied until after I had been accepted. They objected, of course, but by then it was too late. I wanted to get into the war, but most of all, I wanted to see England. I had no intention of staying away for any length of time; it would be more of a visit to do my service and then come back. I boarded the ship in great excitement. It was a childhood dream fulfilled. I was on my way to England.

It was to take 28 days. As we sailed away from the island everything seemed possible, from finding German submarines to seeing King George. We were excited. We did not know what we were getting into. Some English boys back in camp in Jamaica had told me I would like it when I got there, but, once we sailed, I found I was soon missing camp life and the routine.

My time there had been one of hard work and concentration. I had wanted to learn and do my best. The group of boys who joined up with me were all eager to prove themselves. Now on the ship, we were all like overgrown schoolboys. A rumour went round that a German submarine had been sighted. We flew into a panic. But the scare passed and we sailed on to New York.

Here we stopped for a day and people lined the wharfs to cheer us. They were kind. We felt accepted. We felt proud. They called us 'British' boys. We left New York in a convoy of 30 ships. There were nearly 3000 men on our ship. As we sailed into the Atlantic we wrote letters home. I thought of my mother and sisters and the island. I always told my mother whatever I did. I had always been close to her and this parting made me realise my dependence even more. I kept her up-to-date with life on board ship, how the boys played cards and cheated each other, how different the boys from the other islands were.

In mid-Atlantic, one of the English sailors told us it was the graveyard of English shipping and this was the first time a convoy had passed this point without a ship being sunk. The destroyers and escort ships fired their guns in salute. Only a few hours after that, our convoy was attacked. You could see the fire out to sea. We heard over the radio that one of the ships had been attacked and sunk. That frightened us. We lay in our hammocks waiting for a torpedo to come through the side. It was the first time we had seen war, except on the films.

It was October and getting colder. A storm lasted a whole day and a night. A lot of us couldn't eat. The food wasn't what we had been used to. I had never had potato before, not this kind of potato. I had never had a meal without spices. No curry. But we said to ourselves: 'We are men. It is only for a while'. We didn't know then that for some of us it would be years and years.

The second attack was at night. Most of us were asleep. We didn't see much of it, but we heard two ships had been sunk. The next night we were told to be sure not to show any lights on deck. One of the boys wanted us to be attacked again. He wanted to see these Germans for himself. He wanted to get a photograph of a German ship to send to his sister.

The journey seemed endless. It was as if we were going round the world. One minute they said we were going north to Canada, then it would be that we were stopping again in America, and then that we were going to Europe. We thought that maybe the plans were being changed to out do the Germans. But we did not know; no-one told us.

We were happy enough, although there was always a tinge of sadness. We had left home for the first time and for the first time I was with boys rougher than myself. They too were Jamaicans, but they were from other parts of the island. Sometimes there were scuffles. The Jamaicans would fight each other over little things; they also fought the Barbadians, the Trinidadians and the Guianese. Indeed the Jamaicans were everywhere - always the proudest group, always feeling themselves to be the most capable, the strongest and the most intelligent. It is something about the Jamaican, he always feels himself better than the others. He is from the big island, they are from the little ones. The boys from Barbados were timid and gentle, the Trinidad boys were more defiant but generally more friendly to the Jamaicans, the Guianese were somewhere in between. However, it was all new to me. I learned a lot about the West Indies on that journey.

We sailed on and we talked to each other. Foster, a friend I'd joined up with, and Robbie and Martin, who I'd got to know in camp, were together, just the four of us.

On the twenty-seventh day, they announced that we would see England the next day. We stayed up nearly all night. All we could see were shadows, dark clouds, but no England. The air was colder, there was not so much wind and the sea was calm. In the morning we woke up to see the land - land for the first time in so many days. I remember coming up on deck, seeing the coast and running down to tell the boys. Within minutes there were hundreds and hundreds of us looking ashore, but fog was coming up and we soon lost sight of it. It wasn't until night that we really came face to face with England - or, as we soon discovered, Scotland. We arrived in Glasgow harbour and the ship anchored a few miles out. We waited hours for the order to land, but were told to sleep on board that night. The following morning we woke up early and found ourselves tied up in dock. 'This is really it', I thought.

The country was white. I couldn't understand how a country could be so white. Every tree and every house was covered in snow. We put it in our cups and started to eat it, but the sailors told us not to because it was dirty.

It was mid-afternoon before the gangway was opened and we began to land. There were crowds of people to greet us. They waved and cheered and gave us boxes of chocolates, biscuits and cigarettes. They were kind, they were nice people. I felt happy. It was a great country after all, but it was cold! We came off the ship in our thousands and poured into the waiting trains. All along the way through Scotland, people stood and waved to us. Everything was so new and wonderful and we were so proud to be there.

Two

In Camp

In was nearly dark when we arrived at the camp in Yorkshire. My shoes were covered in snow and my feet started to swell. The English sergeant showed us our billet. His first comment was: 'You ought to have your heads tested coming from your hot country to this bloody island. You don't know what it's like. This is only the mild part of the winter. It'll be worse in a month's time'.

From the beginning there was not one word of comfort from the sergeants or the corporals. Maybe it was to stop us getting too optimistic. We went into our billets - long chalets with rows of beds, but oh so cold. There was just one stove in the middle. The boys would gather round and those not strong enough to push their way near the warmth had to stand on the outside and put their hands in their pockets.

I wrote to my mother that night and told her of England, the people, the journey, the camp, the snow. I told her about the English people, who were so white, whiter than those we knew in Jamaica. I couldn't understand that people could be so white and still have blood.

On the third day I went to the post office and asked if I could ship some snow to Jamaica. I was told I could not because it would melt. How I wished my mother could see it. I would have loved to have seen the faces of my sisters as they walked in the snow.

I was very cold. My toes lost all feeling. The sergeant said: 'Don't touch your ears, they'll fall off!' So we never touched them. The wind from the moors cut through us, yet we had to be on parade and we drilled and we marched and we drilled and we marched. We ate boiled potatoes, boiled cabbages, boiled carrots, sometimes boiled beef. There was no taste to any of it. I couldn't drink the tea. I'd never had tea in my life. How I longed for some coffee, but I couldn't get any. We said to the cook: 'We have potato for breakfast, dinner and supper, is there nothing else?'

'You can have bread'. Oh that was really different! How I longed for some rice and curry.

The English soldiers were good fellows, but sergeants are always sergeants. They called us 'black bastards', they called us men with two left feet. 'Hello Sambo'. 'Come here, Blackie'. Every name to do with our colour. But we did not take it seriously. Nobody liked the sergeants anyway. The English soldiers especially. 'Take no notice' they said, 'they call us names too. We are white and they call us 'bloody bastards'. And you being black, they call you 'black bastards'. It doesn't mean anything'.

The sergeants were hard tough men, they'd been in the service for years. They didn't feel the cold. They would drill us without gloves on. I used to wear two pairs of gloves and two pairs of socks. At night we were allowed seven blankets. The CO ordered that we should have more. I had nine issued to me from the stores. We would take it in turns to tuck each other up for the night, but although we were covered in blankets and greatcoats on top, our feet were always cold.

We were three weeks in the camp before anyone told us we could get passes to go to the nearest town, Filey. That evening nearly a thousand were given passes. It was a fantastic sight, crowds of boys swarming on to the buses. I wanted to see the English countryside, an English town with shops. I wished for this so much. I got on the bus and sat next to a corporal.

'You must try the beer', he said.

I told him I didn't want beer. I'd like some rum. He laughed. As we drove into Filey, I could see smoke rising over the town.

'Where's that smoke coming from?', I asked the corporal. 'Is the town on fire?'

'No. It's all the chimneys'.

Chimneys inside houses? I wished I could see one. How could you have a fire in the middle of a house?

We got into Filey and the corporal took me into the first pub we came to. My first time in an English pub. Everyone seemed happy. It was crowded. There were women there as well as men. I hadn't expected that. They all spoke so strangely, I could hardly understand them. It didn't sound like English to me. I wondered if they were foreigners.

The woman behind the bar gave us beer. The way she pulled the beer from under the counter fascinated me. She pulled a lever and up came a glass of beer. I asked the corporal if she would show me and she let me go round the bar to see how she did it. Then the corporal told her I was curious about chimneys and asked if I might see her fireplace. She was very kind and took me to see it. There for the first time I saw a room with a fire in it. Such an important place, so warm - it was actually inside the house yet there was no mess and no danger. I sketched it on a bit of paper to send home to my mother. I also sketched the bar to show her. Back home the bars were so very different.

At that time, we didn't feel different from any other stranger in a new country. The question of colour never entered my head. They were English, I was Jamaican. I was in the services and so were they, or most of them seemed to be. If their skin was white, it was because they had no sun. But as I walked along the street with Robbie later that evening, we noticed little children lining up to watch us. Again we thought it must be because we were new. Then they began asking us the time, so naturally we told them. They asked so regularly that we wondered if they were not yet able to tell the time by a clock. I asked a passing civilian and he said they were curious to find out if we spoke English. We thought that was very funny. Then the buses arrived and we went back to camp. I had been impressed by the fireplace and the pub, but nothing else in that town impressed me. It was dreary and cold and all the buildings were shut up.

In camp I was neither happy nor sad, just not sure of what was happening around me. But as the months went by I began to make more contact. The Jamaicans were billeted separately from the Barbadians and Trinidadians. One morning the Jamaicans in one billet decided they would not go on parade because it was too cold. They barricaded themselves in, so three of us were asked to go over and talk to them. We told them we were all in the services now; if we could go out in the snow then so could they. A lot of them wanted to go home, but then so did we all, but none of us could. Eventually the CO had to come over and talk to them. Then the boys came out, back into the slush, the ice, the muck and the cold wind. My ears burned in the cold. I wandered about in the evening praying that the sea would dry up and working out how long it would take me to walk home. I really didn't want to stay.

The months went by. We queued up for a letter, but if one didn't arrive, our whole world collapsed. There was nothing happy in me. All my childhood dreams seemed to be frozen in this ice box. The snow fell, the wind blew. In the canteen it was the same old boiled food, cabbage so coarse it was like eating rough blankets. We held a meeting and decided to ask for some rice. We were promised that rice would come. Eventually it arrived - we even had curry once or twice.

The time came for our passing out parade and we waited to be posted. It was late March before the snow began to melt and the sun came out. Soon we saw green leaves. We made good friends with the English soldiers We went out drinking. I was still 'Eric'. I was not yet a 'black man'. Simply I was Jamaican, they were English. There was no obvious problem.

I was posted to Barford St Michael and was there six weeks when I met an English girl for the first time. She was telling me about the town and where to buy things, but she looked curious.

'Why do you look like that?' I asked.

'Your teeth are so white'.

I didn't say anything.

'Are all the boys from Jamaica as dark as you?'.

I told her we were all different colours.

'Is it because of the sun that you get so dark?'

I couldn't answer. We had always lived in the sun. I didn't know.

'Would you like to come and see my father? He's always wanted to see a black man'.

I said: 'No. I don't think I would like to see your father'.

'Please come!'

I thought she was direct, very matter of fact, but so cold. There was nothing warm in her voice. In fact she was really rather innocent, she didn't mean any harm. It was just the way she said things that worried me a bit. I didn't understand why she should ask me about my colour. I expected her to know that people from the West Indies are black and brown. Maybe no-one had told her. I didn't want to go and show her father what a black man looked like. But she made me wonder. When I got back to camp I told Ben, an English boy I'd got to know. He said people round here had never seen black people before; they were curious and a bit ignorant and that I must not take any notice. He was quite reassuring. He handled it very well.

Ben was a good chap. We had a drink from time to time and went to the pictures. He told me about his parents. They lived in London. He told me how he went to the speedway track and motorbike racing, which I liked myself. Life began to be a bit easier because of Ben. I felt closer to England. Up to now I'd been with Jamaicans and never really mixed. He told me about his girl friends. Many times he tried to make a date for me, but I never went.

We were posted together to an army camp in Buckinghamshire to go on a course in the Royal Army Medical Corps. Ben said it was near London and he would like to take me there. I was thrilled as I wanted to see London. I felt so good. Ben said we could stay with his family. We had ten days leave to come the following month. I wrote to my mother that I was invited to an English home and Ben was taking me to London. My mother wrote back delighted and asked me to send a photograph. Ben gave me one and I sent it to her.

Three

In London with Ben

Ben and I hitch-hiked to London. I wanted to see everything - all in one day. Ben said it would take months it was so big and there was a lot of walking to do. It was odd that when we arrived Ben didn't take me straight to his home. We went to a YMCA hostel. I thought maybe his family were away on holiday, but I wondered. That evening we went to the pictures and afterwards I asked Ben.

'I think we are better off spending a few days by ourselves first. I want to surprise them. We'll see as much as we can and then we'll go home. You know how parents are. They won't let you out of their sight, so we'll have some fun first'.

I accepted this. It seemed reasonable. We went to the dog track, to Wembley to see the Harlem Globe Trotters, to Buckingham Palace, to Windsor and to Tower Bridge. I saw so much, it was wonderful. It seemed endless. There was so much to write home - letters and letters to my family. Then on the Saturday evening Ben said: 'There's a pub I used to go to near my house. We'll go there, have a drink and then go home'.

The lady behind the bar was kind, although she did call me 'Sambo'. She offered me a drink on the house, which I thought was nice. 'You're always welcome here' she said. This I did think strange. I had supposed that everyone was welcome in a pub. We had our drinks. Ben was gloomy. I tried telling him stories about the boys, but they did not seem to register. Then he said suddenly: 'You see that man over there in the cap? That's my father'.

'Your father? Well, aren't you going to talk to him?'

'When I've finished my drink'.

He did finish his drink and then went over to his father. I watched them both talking and looking over at me. Then they came over.

'Dad, this is Eric, the friend I told you about. This is the man you refused to have home. Look at him, shake his hand. Go on shake his hand. He doesn't bite!'

His father's head dropped. I felt bad, as if I could go through the floor. My whole world crumbled. The women behind the bar tried to cheer me.

'Never mind, we like you. Some people are so stupid about black men. Take no notice, you can come here any time you want'.

All this was just background noise to me, all I could think was: Why doesn't his father want so see me? What have I done? In a curious way I felt guilty, as if I was in the wrong. Then I heard Ben's father's voice: 'Pleased to meet you. I don't hate you, why should I? I don't know you. Never seen you before. Take no notice of my son. He's had too much to drink'.

'No I haven't' Ben said, 'you wrote and told me not to bring him. I've got the letter in my pocket. You know damn well! I wrote and told you about him. How do you think I felt when you wrote and told me not to bring him? I didn't know how to tell him. I never told him. But I thought we shouldn't go back without letting him know the truth'.

Everyone in the pub was now listening. The woman came from behind the bar and put her arm around me. 'This country's got some funny people in it. But we aren't all like it. You mustn't let it upset you. There's good and bad everywhere?'

She was trying to help, but I just stood there shocked, suddenly disillusioned, somehow guilty. I didn't know what to say, where to look. I didn't know why I felt so anxious. Ben's father went back to his friends, but before he went he said to Ben: 'You can bring your friend round to meet your mother tomorrow. See you at home'.

Ben and I left the pub and took the bus back to the YMCA. Along the way we didn't talk. We went up to our room and he sat down on the bed and wept.

'You know how parents are' I said, echoing his earlier words. I told him a story about my own father. Once I took an Indian boy to the house and my father did not like it. I had been very angry with him and he forbade me to bring the boy again. But it didn't help Ben.

'This is England. We are fighting a war about these things. The Germans are supposed to be the ones who hate. We are supposed to be different'.

He was angry and bitter and said he wanted to die.

'No point in dying' I said. Here I was trying to cheer up this boy whose father had just insulted me. Something crazy somewhere. Ben went to bed. I couldn't sleep. I thought about home and family, the sunshine and all the good things we had. I looked at myself in the mirror. I looked at my hands, my face and I became very conscious of myself, conscious that there was a difference. It wasn't just being Jamaican, Trinidadian, Tobagan or English. I was a 'coloured' man. Now it was here and real. I went out and walked the streets and began noticing people. They had stared before but now I was supremely conscious of their stares. This awareness was frightening. The danger was that this new awareness could so easily make me misinterpret honest statements, friendly intentions and curiosity. I told myself it must not affect me.

Next morning Ben said we could go home to his family.

'Why should I' I said.

'Don't be a bloody fool. Come and show them you're better than they are'.

I wondered if I was even good enough. But we went. His mother and sister were there: his sister very cheerful, his mother quiet and older than I had expected. She greeted me.

'Come in and sit down. Let me take your coat. I heard all about last night. Ben you were naughty to talk to your father like that in front of people'.

To me: 'We don't hate anyone. You mustn't get it wrong. People round here are just not used to coloured people and they would talk if they saw a coloured man come into our house. So we thought rather than embarrass you we'd tell Ben not to bring you. Anyway, that's all past and you're here. Now, what will you have to eat?'

It turned out to be very pleasant. We stayed about three days. We were out most of the time, Ben's sister came with us. His father was friendly but all along I had a suspicion that he was just putting up with me. They were polite and cheerful but I did not feel close. I was aware of the distance and could feel the rejection.

We went back to camp and life went on as usual. But I had a lot on my mind. My biggest worry was whether I should write it in a letter home. It was the first time I had something to hide. For days I thought about it. If I told my mother she would be sure to say she was right, that I shouldn't have joined up and left home. But more than that, it would upset her. I couldn't put it in a letter. I could never let them know.

Soon after Ben was sent out to the Far East, but he kept writing and I wrote back. He often wrote about his parents and sent me their best regards. His sister invited me to their home again. I went once on a weekend leave. Then somehow I lost contact for about two years. Suddenly one day I had a letter from Ben's father asking me to come to his wife's funeral in place of Ben. I was very upset to hear she was dead and astonished by the invitation. I got a few days leave and attended the funeral. It was so different from those back home. I thought it very solemn and dignified, but the service was so short.

I didn't feel like a stranger, I felt I knew this family now. I went back to camp and thought about it more. After such an unhappy first meeting, I had been honoured to be at the funeral in place of a son who was far away.

His father had said to me: 'She can see you now. She's very proud of you, just as she would have been had you been her son'.

Yet it had all started with a flash of racial prejudice that had shocked and frightened me because it was the first time I had ever really experienced it.

Four

Innocence and Ignorance

Up in Cumberland the camp was near a small town by the sea. There were only a few Jamaicans there. One hot afternoon four of us were lazing around on the beach when two children came by, a boy about eleven and a girl a few years younger. They stared at us very hard but didn't say anything. We were gazing out to sea, happy to feel the sun on our faces. They came back and stared again, but still didn't say anything. The little girl was obviously longing to speak, but the boy took her hand and pulled her away. Then they passed by again; this time they stopped and she said: 'Hello'.

'Hello' I said.

'You see!' She turned to the boy: 'He does speak English'.

'Yes' I said.

'And you wear clothes'.

'Yes'.

'And you wear shoes'.

My friends got impatient: 'Why do you answer all these questions?'

'Well if she thought we didn't wear clothes and didn't speak English now she's finding out it was wrong and she's learning something. I don't see why we shouldn't help her'.

'Our teacher told us that black men live in trees and they don't wear shoes and they don't wear clothes and they don't have houses'.

'You can tell your teacher now that you met some black men who do wear shoes and clothes'.

My friends were furious now. Why should we educate these stupid kids just because their teacher was ignorant? The children ran away and we started a big argument. Don't people here know that black men wear clothes and speak English? Surely they know about their own Empire? It's theirs, isn't it? Don't they know the difference between the dominions and the colonies? Don't they know how we got here? Are the teachers really so ignorant or do they tell the children lies? We were angry with the teachers but I couldn't be angry with the children.

The first words a little niece of an English friend said to me were: 'Don't you ever wash?'

'Yes', I said.

'But if you wash why is you skin so black?'

'If there was dirt on my skin I would wash and it would come off, same as yours'.

'But my skin isn't black when I've washed it'.

I took off my shoe and went to the sink and washed it. 'There you see, if you wash the dirt off your shoe it's still black'.

'But your skin isn't leather like your shoe'.

'Some skins are darker than others, but that doesn't mean they are dirty'.

My friend was angry with his niece and thought she should not ask these questions. But it seemed to me that perhaps only we ourselves can teach people who don't know, especially children. If they do not know they ask directly and you can tell them and not feel hurt. With adults it can be disguised and unexpectedly cruel.

I was having supper with an English couple and we talked all evening about politics and the way of life in the West Indies. Afterwards, when the husband took me to the bus stop he said: 'By the way, what language do you normally speak?' I felt terribly insulted. I found such little incidents very upsetting. I was becoming over-sensitive because it was happening so often. I asked myself how people could be so ignorant. That same night the bus conductor asked me what part of Africa Jamaica was in. I said: 'Just north of Egypt'. I was so angry. Surely he was being sarcastic? He couldn't be telling me he just didn't know?

I went back to camp and thought about ignorance and

innocence. It was difficult to distinguish between the two. Our expectation of the English was higher than the reality. We expected them to know their own history. When they showed us they didn't, we felt disappointed in them, and angry to be asked such stupid questions. We got used to statements like: 'How can you leave your beautiful island? There's so much sunshine there. It must be wonderful'. They knew nothing about Jamaica, yet we knew so much about England. I knew the geography of every county and had some knowledge of every big town, I could recite the kings and queens of England from the beginning. But they seemed to know nothing about the Empire. They forgot there was a war on and we were in it with them because it was our war too. Years later I began to understand the difference between ignorance and innocence. With the ignorant, prejudice is a way of life. They don't like the Scots, or the Welsh, or the Irish, or the Jews. They don't like the rich or the poor and they don't like the clever. They are far more dangerous than the innocent. I learned to pick out the innocent and could deal with them apparently just as innocently. But the ignorant cause violence by the way they say things. I got into several fights with the ignorant, generally soldiers, usually Americans.

Inside myself, I searched for the reasons for the violence, for the state of the world. The ignorance of the people, being coloured, being bitter, doubtful and suspicious, these were matters that confronted me day-in day-out.

In a pub in Somerset a man came up and said: 'What colour is your blood? Is it red or is it black?'

I ignored him. It was the kind of question that brought out my fury. If I didn't react he might go away and I could dismiss it. But he insisted. He put his hand next to mine and compared the colour. He repeated his question. I pushed him aside and knocked his beer over. That started it. We struck each other again and again until a policeman separated us. This is the way trouble starts, a low stupid statement meant to hurt. I was ready to ignore it, not to respond, but he meant to hurt. Two Scots boys from the camp joined in the fight. It turned into a very interesting evening. They stood by me because we were from the same camp and were in uniform although we had not met before. Now my loneliness soon vanished because here were people of the same race not just attacking but also defending me. Once you experience this support you feel you are not alone. With everyone against you, it is easy to resort to violence, but in this instance those two lads who came forward helped me turn what could have been an ugly fight into a mere scuffle. The pain of cutting rejection changed to exhilaration. The policeman warned us to be careful and then he went off. We all shook hands and had another beer, and the fellow said: 'Maybe I did push it a bit far'.

One evening in camp I was losing at poker. I usually did. One of the boys was cheating. A fellow called Joe who sat next to me closed his hand and said he would not play any more. Then he looked at my hand and helped me to play it. The next round he helped me again. In fact, he played it for me and I won thirty shillings, which was about five shillings over what I had lost. He then advised me to stop playing. These boys were sharp and would take all the money I had. I thought that was good of him. I did not know him, had never spoken to him before, but he helped me out because he could see I was being cheated, and this was important to me. We left the game and he asked me what I was doing that evening. I said I'd not thought about it. He wanted to go out for a drink but he had only a few shillings left. I said: 'I've got what you helped me to win back. The drinks are on me'.

From then on we became good friends, helped each other if we were pushed out of the queue at mealtimes and we told each other about our parents and our homes. He told me about his girl friends and he used to invite me to make up a foursome. A few other boys joined in with us, the two Scots boys who had helped me out in the put that time, and another two boys from Wales. One night we went out and Joe got talking to a girl in a pub. Joe and I sat with this girl at one table and the others sat at the next one. A fellow came in and turned on the girl.

'I've only got to turn my back a minute and you're out with a nigger!'

The girl flashed back: 'Don't be so stupid. Who do you think you are anyway?'

'I'm an Englishman and proud of it'.

Joe jumped up at that. 'And I'm a bloody Englishman too, you bastard!'

They went for each other. I tried to separate them but this fellow had some friends in the pub and as soon as I got up they started on me. Our mates at the next table joined in. Quite a to do. Eventually we were all thrown out. The girl came with us. Joe said to me: 'That sort are no different from the Germans. I hate the bastards. You stick with me. We'll show 'em. You're a thousand times better than they are'.

The girl did not say much and seemed sad. Then she and Joe began to talk. She said people like that were just jealous and ignorant and she hoped I wouldn't take any notice of them. A lot of people were like that. As soon as they saw an English girl talking to a coloured man they got the wrong idea. But I wasn't to worry about it.

Joe and I got ourselves into a lot of situations like this. He always stood up for me and we were always together inside and outside the camp. He and the others we'd teamed up with made life in Somerset quite eventful.

Five

Angry Days in London and Swansea

Peace returned to England. Everything was in a muddle and the people, free from the war, were anxious to rebuild their homes and towns. I went back to London on leave a few months before being demobbed. I had been in England three years now. I had grown up. I was aware, conscious of myself, lonely, angry, frustrated. I went back to London expecting the worst, and I got it. Later I wondered if I had expected the best would I have got that instead? But I had no reason to hope for the best. I thought bitterly of the first time. How excited I'd been at the prospect of seeing the great old city, the centre of the world we had learned about at school. My world had been shattered that first time. This time I was alone and looking for somewhere to sleep. I went to the first hotel I saw in Russell Square and was told there was no bed. I believed the man, but just as I went to the door a Canadian soldier about my age came in and asked if they had a bed. The man said they had. I didn't walk out. Events over the months had destroyed my meekness. I was angry and I felt cheated. I went back to the desk.

'Why did you tell me there were no beds and this chap comes in and gets one?'

The Canadian turned to me. 'You were refused a bed?' And he turned back to the man. 'Keep your bloody bed!' And he snatched the register he had just signed and threw it on the floor. The man rang a bell and two porters appeared. They tried to throw us out but they did not succeed until we had thrown everything off the desk on to the floor. Then we went to a YMCA. We couldn't get a bed there either, they were genuinely full up. So we decided to walk the streets instead.

About eleven we went into a restaurant in Camden Town. There were four other Jamaicans there. We sat down near them and they told us they had been waiting hours to get served. The waitress was serving other people. She was certainly busy but when half an hour went by we realised that she was just ignoring us. The Canadian went up and ordered a meal for all of us. She told him to mind his own business. He threatened her and she took the order but refused to bring the food to the table. The Canadian brought it to us. People in the restaurant watched it all. We paid for the meal but we could not eat it. Our stomachs were full. So we kicked the tables over and threw the food all over the place. People were shouting now and running out of the restaurant. The police came. Some of us were held and some got away. We didn't get charged; we were just warned. They told us we might get a bill for damages but it never came.

I went to Clapham South by tube one evening to meet another Jamaican. He was staying some way from the station and I had to take a bus. I stood at the bus stop for over an hour. Three buses passed but never stopped. A fourth bus came and by now an Englishwoman was waiting at the stop. She got on and the conductor put his arm across and said: 'No more!' So I had to walk. I was a 'coloured' man. I never found my friend's address and went back across the river.

This kind of frustration continued. I was sure people were staring at me more than ever. More people seemed to be saying to me: 'Why are you still here? Why don't you go home?' I began to ask myself why not. Why did I stay? I didn't know the answer. Something seemed to be holding me here. I was hoping that some day, sooner or later, these same people would see that I was just as good as they, that there was much we had to solve together.

Once, on another trip to London, six of us were approached by two men who said they were making a film. They offered us twenty pounds each and took us to a house in north London and asked us to strip and put on loin cloths. They gave us paint for our faces. They wanted us to look like Africans, like 'jungle men', they said, and they wanted us to look the real thing. We could have done with the money but we refused to humiliate ourselves for it. They raised it to twenty five pounds. We told them we were Jamaicans. If they wanted to make a film about the jungle they should go to the jungle and make it. We left the studio.

It seemed everything and everyone was full of deceit. Surely it couldn't go on like this? But this is how it went on. It never changed.

Two of us went into a pub and asked for two beers. My friend asked for a brown beer and got a bitter. He reminded the barman he had asked for a brown.

'Why the hell don't you speak English then?'

'I just asked for a brown beer'.

'Don't you shout at me!'

'I'm not shouting. I just asked for a brown beer'.

'Why the hell don't you go back up the trees? If you have to speak like you come from the jungle why don't you go back there?'

'My friend asked for a brown beer' I said, 'You heard him but you are so angry that you don't want to understand him'.

He started screaming at both of us then and told us to get out. We left. There was nothing we could do. Sometimes we were too damned tired of the whole business to keep fighting back. It was too big, too tough. There had to be another way.

One time I met an American soldier at the YMCA, a black American. I'd never met anyone so angry with white people, English, Europeans, Americans, all of them. He told me he had had fights all over Germany and France with his own countrymen. He showed me some German guns he had captured.

'If you can't get away, can't be accepted, shoot your way through them'.

'I don't need your guns' I said, 'These people here just don't know us and they ought to know us, and we've got to help them understand us. Guns can only kill'.

They kill quickly and for no reason. One Saturday night a few of us had been eating in an Indian restaurant in Goodge Street where Jamaican servicemen usually gathered. Some fellows came in with their girls from a dancehall which was also a meeting place for Jamaicans. We were all soon to be demobbed and were in great spirits. Everyone was happy and relaxed. There must have been about thirty of us and a few English as well, all in uniform except for two Englishmen at one table. The waitress was rushing about trying to serve us all. We were in no hurry, just happy to be together and talk about going home. But the two English civilians were getting impatient. One got up and shouted at the girl: 'We've been here for nearly fifteen minutes and you haven't even taken our order yet!'

'Give us a chance', the girl said, 'I've got all these others with orders before you. I'll come to you in turn'.

The English chaps wouldn't have it. I remembered the times when I waited to be served in a restaurant. This time it was the English who were waiting. The girl went on serving and on one of her many journeys with a trayful of food she passed these two fellows and one put his foot out. She tripped over and fell and spilled the food all over the floor. She was furious. She got up and shouted at these two. One of them reached up and pushed her forward.

'Who the hell do you think you are, serving these blacks before us?'

'If you don't like it get out!'

We sat on at our tables, quiet now, and waited. The two English civvies went on shouting, calling her all the dirty names they could think of. One of us, a strong serious fellow, finally got up and ambled over to the Englishmen's table.

'Leave her alone, She is only doing her job. You don't have to insult her'.

The Englishmen didn't answer. They got up and walked out. The manager came and the floor was cleaned up and we settled back to our food and the evening went on. At one corner table were two Jamaicans due to return home on the first boat. They were brothers and this was the first time they had met for over two years. They had been split up and sent to different camps for most of the time they'd been in England. They were the first to get up and leave the restaurant. As one opened the door to go out a gun was fired.

Two shots were heard, it happened so quickly. He fell backwards, and his brother saved his fall and we went to help. We picked him up and brought him to one of the tables. As he lay on the table he tried to say something but before he could say it he just died. It was very sad. It was sad because he had served four years in a strange country in a war without being wounded. It was sad because he was going home on the first boat out. It was sad because he had just met up with his brother after so long. It was sad because he was shot and he was dead.

We were all silent as these thoughts came to us. Then we got angry. The waitress said: 'It was those two fellows. I know it. I'm sure of it'.

The police came and warned us not to do anything rash. We insisted that we knew what they looked like. We could find them quicker than the police. After a lot of argument the police officer gave in and said: 'All right, go ahead and find them. But no fights mind. Don't harm them. Just bring them in to the nearest police station'.

It was like a fire let loose in a high wind. All the Jamaicans in London took it upon themselves to search the city. We went to every cafe, every bar, every dancehall, every YMCA; we called out the boys and we all searched. We looked everywhere but nowhere could we find them. We went to bed sad. We tried to console the brother. There was hate in us, and regret, and there was sadness. We were sick, sick of this country, sick of everything. We couldn't understand. Every day seemed worse, every day seemed more confused, more full of conflict. And now death. What next, we asked ourselves.

The two men were found eventually. It was the waitress who informed the police. She had a friend who knew one of the men. I'm sure it was her acceptance of us that made her come forward, but that didn't come out in the trial. The two men denied they had shot the boy but they admitted to having a gun. When the case was first tried the court was so crowded with Jamaicans that many of us had to stand outside. And when we felt the case would go against us we all put what money we had together and got enough to send to Jamaica for a lawyer. A Mr Manley KC was asked to come over. He said he would come to the Old Bailey, but he would not want any money. The two men were convicted. The jury wanted to let them go on the grounds that there was insufficient evidence, but Mr Manley managed to get a verdict of technical guilt and they were sentenced to ten years each.

This was some justice for us, but a lot of us were not satisfied. At that time, the death sentence was in force in England and most of us felt they should have been hanged. We didn't feel that ten years in prison was adequate for the unnecessary killing of an innocent boy who just wanted to go home with his brother. But these things happen and this is how you feel when you belong to a minority deprived group in a larger powerful society. Every wrong is the greater because you are the victim, and the wound is more painful because you feel it and there can be no redress.

Guns can only kill. There had to be another way.

Most of the good folk I knew were British servicemen, the Jocks and Paddys and Geordies and Taffys, boys who had joined up like me and now had hopes of making a new life out of the mess. We went around together. Sometimes I went home with them.

I remember one family who was very good to me. We were sitting round talking one evening when a friend of the family came in. His first comment was: 'Isn't it dark in here'. I didn't know what he meant. The room was bright enough. It wasn't until after I left that house that I realised he was talking about me. My blackness darkened the house. I said to myself I mustn't let him and his kind put me off. He wouldn't keep me from the English people. He wouldn't keep me from my friends.

Two English friends invited me to meet their families and as we sat in the garden on a sunny afternoon a neighbour joined us. We talked about the coloured troops and somebody raised the question of rejection, that it was so stupid that we were not accepted. This neighbour turned to me with a confidential yet distant look and said: 'They don't really accept you fellows.

They don't really like you. None of them. They tolerate you because you are British. I don't know why the hell you want to be British because they don't really want you. Why don't you fellows get wise and go home. You came here, you fought and died with us. We'd have won the war without you anyway. I don't know why you came. Because now it's all over they don't want you. No offence to you personally mind, you're intelligent, you're one of the educated ones. Any time you want you can come to my house. But I know some who wouldn't have you'.

I listened on. My hosts were embarrassed, but I wasn't worried. I was amazed at his honesty. There was a lot of truth in what he said. But because it was true and unpleasant it didn't mean I had to rise up against him. Maybe we had been used. We believed we had been contributing to the war effort, that we had some purpose in being here. We'd been used the world over for centuries. It was nothing unusual to be told so. I was getting accustomed to being shouted at, insulted, rejected and, sometimes, protected by white people.

When I was stationed in South Wales two English boys took me to a pub in Swansea. It was my turn for a round and I went up to the bar to get some beer. Some Americans at the bar said to the barman: 'Don't serve the bloody nigger'. The barman said quietly: 'This is Wales. This isn't America. And he's British'.

'You British, you stink! You don't know how to treat niggers!'

The barman quietly pulled my beers and set them in front of me. One of the Americans pushed them off the bar, broke the glasses and spilled the beer over me. An English soldier who I didn't know and who had been sitting just behind, suddenly leaped up and hit the American in the eyes.

'Go back to your own bloody country and leave him alone! He's one of ours. Go and hit your own!'

That sparked off a real fight and eventually the Americans were thrown out of the pub. The English stranger called me over.

'Have a drink with me. And bring your two mates. Yankee bastards! Think they own the bloody country!'

Fellows like him were genuine. I didn't see it as just sympathy, certainly not patronising. It was just an honest straightforward reaction to injustice. And the barman had real courage. He knew what was right and he stood by it even if it meant a fight in his pub and losing American customers. Strange people, these British. Here I was in London being refused hotel rooms, being refused service in cafes, not allowed on the bus; yet I was in a Swansea pub with a barman saying why shouldn't I drink with the rest of them. Somebody else was saying it, not me, and ready to fight for it too. People like him and the English soldier and the Canadian in London and the gang down in Somerset made it easier for me to stand the many rejections. This was so important for me. If I was to survive in this country I had to feel good about the people, even though I doubted I would ever understand them. But I had to feel they would accept me, that I had the right to walk, breathe, eat and drink with them, to be a man and human.

They were the ones who gave me the inner strength to stay and mix, to live and be iike everyone else. Gradually my confidence would be restored and the tensions would disappear. I could begin to meet rejection without fear and disillusion.

Six

The Good House in Doncaster

There was an hour to wait at Doncaster for the train to Hull. I left
the station and went out into the town to find a bookshop. A girl
in her twenties stopped me hesitantly in the street and asked:
'Are you Jamaican?'
'Yes', I said.
'I'm so pleased'.
I didn't know what she meant but it certainly was a change
for someone to be pleased to see me.
'My mother would like to meet you. She has been longing to
meet a Jamaican. Promise me you will go and see her'.
'I can't. My train leaves in little more than an hour and I have
some friends waiting for me in Hull'.
'We only live a fourpenny bus ride away. There's plenty of
time. Try your best and go. She will be disappointed if you don't
turn up'.
She gave me an address card and walked off. I stood looking
after her, the card in my hand. I would never understand these
people. In London there were some who wouldn't serve me or
let me ride on a bus, and in Doncaster here was a girl saying I
must go and meet her mother. I looked at my watch. What
should I do? Two Jamaicans were sitting in the window of a cafe
across the street. I went over and asked them about Doncaster
and the buses. They told me the only thing they knew about it
was the camp where they were stationed. I showed them the

address card and told them the story and asked if one of them would go instead of me. 'They'll never know the difference', I said.

'It's your treasure, man. Go and reap it' they said.

So I took the bus and found the house. It was beautiful, standing far back and high from the road. When you got to the gate you had to look up to find the steps up to the door. As I went up a little old lady came out and stood at the top. She held my hand and embraced me and said: 'You're the Jamaican. I'm so pleased. Come on inside'.

Still puzzled I followed her. 'Come in here. This is the library. Make yourself at home and I'll get you a drink'.

She went out and I looked around the shelves. All the books seemed to be about Jamaica. This just puzzled me even more. It seemed like some sort of dream. As soon as she came back I asked her why she wanted to meet a Jamaican.

'There's plenty of time for that'.

'There's no time. I've only half an hour now to get my train'.

'Oh, I've taken care of that. You're not going to Hull on that train because I've already telephoned the station and told them to look after your kitbag. You're going to stay with us'.

'But I have some friends waiting to meet me'.

'They must wait'.

I couldn't get my way. She was in charge and she just told me what she wanted. But I wanted to stay because I was curious and this was the first time I had been in an English house of this size. She took me into the dining room and her husband came in, a business man of about seventy. I still didn't know why I was there. The girl came in too. She was a school teacher she said. And we sat down for lunch. The old lady was apologetic. 'I haven't got Jamaican food ready for lunch. There wasn't time. But this evening I shall cook some myself'.

And we chatted on through lunch and through the long afternoon about Jamaica. And still no-one would tell me why I was there. I looked at my watch again.

'I must get the train'.

'You can't leave us now. I want you to stay a day or two'.

'I've got ten days leave and I was going to stay with my friends in Hull'.

'You can take your holiday here. You can write and tell them'.

I couldn't resist the old lady. She was so charming, so insistent, so sure I would stay. I had never met anyone like her. And I felt curiously at peace, even though I still had no idea why she wanted me to stay. But somebody was at last accepting me as I was, a Jamaican. I was not a 'coloured' man, no-one was asking if I could speak English, no-one was asking why didn't I go back to the jungle.

That evening she cooked a meal such as I had not had since I left home: chicken curry, red beans, and rice with real Jamaican rum. After dinner she took me into the garden and sat me down in a chair.

'Now I will tell you why you are here. I promised myself that I would entertain the first Jamaican I met in my own house. My two sons are in Jamaica and they have been treated so well by your people I thought the least I could do to repay them was to give one of you men the same'.

She showed me pictures of her sons and told me they were in the shipping business. So that was it. I thought of those two boys in the cafe who said it was my treasure, go and reap it. Maybe this would be a turning point for me.

I spent all my leave in that house. Those ten days were the happiest time I'd had since I left home. I met their friends, was taken to parties, went walking in the country. I learned to go to bed early after listening to the nine o'clock news. I learned to listen to the piano after dinner, to have a nap after lunch. I learned you could sit and read all afternoon without caring. There was so much difference between this house and the others I'd been in. These must be the real English that I had only just found. Maybe I just wanted to think so. If these were the real English who were all those others in London, the ones who shouted and stared at me? Was it the education that made the difference? Or the money? I never had an answer. Whatever it was it served its purpose well. I was happy and they made me feel welcome.

As I left the house I felt full of good things. They took me to the station and saw me off. I kept up correspondence with them for years afterwards and they sent me books and parcels. Eventually we lost contact, but they did good service to my thoughts. They helped me to know the good things about this country, the people, the gentle way of life. They proved my belief that there are people who will accept you as you are, with the same feelings, the same need for understanding and warmth, who want you to live among them and be one of them.

On the long journey back to camp I was full of these thoughts. Others would be like this. My long anger was gone. I felt new and ready to begin again. I wrote to my mother that night, the first time for many months. I had something good to write.

Seven

The Learning Time

The good times helped me to survive the bad times, but the bad times taught me more. I look back now on my life in the RAF as the years of learning, through all the rejections, the persecution, the fears and the shame. All the people I met, in London and all over the island, the experiences we shared, taught me to survive - not just to survive, but to grow and live. Perhaps they learned something from me too. I cannot tell because all through these years I never talked deeply to anyone about what was happening to me.

As a child I used to go to church. My mother was very religious and insisted that we all go to church. On my first Sunday in England, up in the camp in Yorkshire, I went to church as I had always done. On the second Sunday, one of the English boys asked me to join in a game of cards. I said no, I was going to church. Some of the others heard me and they laughed, quite kindly, and said: 'You've got a long way to go before you catch up'. I didn't know what they meant. 'You're fifty years behind the times', they said. 'We've passed that stage here. No-one goes to church in England any more. That's why you've got all those missionaries out there'. They laughed again. And they said: 'In this part of the world we don't love our neighbours any more. We shoot them if they don't behave. That's why you're here. That's why we're all here in this bloody camp. You've got a lot to learn, boy'.

Somehow I began to believe them, I began to see no value in the church in England. The ministers said the same words as they did at home. We were all God's children, equal and loved. But outside the church I was black, alone, and 'unbelonging'. Didn't the ministers know that? I started to question the things they taught me. I didn't believe in them any more. I couldn't write home about these things. Only once when I was very down, did I try to explain how it was to my mother, the one person who had always been my closest confidante. Years later I came across my letter carefully preserved among her belongings.

'This month makes it three years since I came to England', I wrote: 'So much has happened since I left. You must not worry too much or think the worst when I tell you that you were right when you said I should not have joined up. I feel I must tell you this because it has been on my mind for so long now. England is not what I thought it would be. It is so cold and wet and everyday I feel more alone. I miss Jamaica and all of you very much. In your last letter you said I should keep away from the rough boys and make some good English friends. I know now, Mother, why the boys are rough and I cannot help being with them, but every time I remember what you wrote. They get into trouble but sometimes they cannot help it. I have made friends with two Scottish boys, Jock W... and Jock L..., and a Welsh boy called Taffy. They have been good to me since I lost Ben. But when they go on leave to their homes I am alone again. I don't know what's right any more. I cannot tell you everything because I don't want to worry you. I am not in any danger and I am well, but I am so confused. Sometimes I want to die, I'm so homesick. You said I should go to church. I do go but there is no comfort there. This is a big country, Mother, and so different I cannot begin to tell you. I will never join anything again. I try hard to forget many things but I cannot. Mother, you cannot understand. If only I were home I could tell you. But I am trying my best. And it won't be long now before they send us home...'

She wrote back at once, very worried and upset. And I resolved then that I would never again try to write these things in a letter. From then on the family only heard the good things. I thought of my grandfather, the years he had spent fighting in two wars for this country, and my father who had been in the

First World War. Did they believe they were fighting for freedom, for the homeland, the Empire? My war seemed to be very different. I wasn't sure what it was about, but my battle seemed to be with the homeland and I knew some of it was inside me. My thoughts were never the same, they were changing as I came to new things, new places, new people. In younger days I enjoyed violence. I would be with the boys and feel strong and protected. I didn't care. We could always punch our way through. We could be together, get our food in the Indian restaurants and keep out of the way of the English. But in my heart I didn't want this. I wanted the English to let me in.

I keep good memories of the RAF, especially of the boys in the ranks like me. I did not feel offended when the sergeants called me a black bastard. They were sergeants. They had three stripes on their arms to say what they wanted. But it was hard when it came from others. I couldn't take it. But I willed myself that if I was going to stay I must put up with it. I tolerated it for years and I am still not convinced that the people who insult me are any less human than I. I know they are ignorant and I wish they would learn, I believe they can learn. And it is this belief that helped me to stay, and to tolerate, and perhaps to teach if they would let me. I am wiser and more sure than I would have been if I had stayed in Jamaica. I know the meaning of what it is to be black in a white country and I learned how to make use of my understanding.

To integrate was a challenge and I feared it. Could I integrate in this country? I could not be sure that I would ever overcome the doubts, mine and everyone else's. Now, over forty years later, I am still not sure. But I have learned many things.

I learned to recognise two kinds of rejection. There is the face-to-face rejection and there is an indirect kind. You go up to talk to people in a room, maybe at a party or in a pub. One fellow turns his back as you walk up and it is only when the person you are talking to calls to him that he turns round, so surprised, and says: 'Oh hello! It's you Eric!' And all along he saw you, he knew you were there. And you feel the rage rising, but you smile. And it is harder for you than the direct insult.

The things that happened left their mark. Always being

talked about. Always talked about as being 'coloured'. What are you doing here? Always being reminded of my status, and that, in the eyes of those who gave it to me, I was inferior. I got tired of the way some people found it necessary to be over kind. 'Never mind Eric. Take no notice'. It was the wrong kind of reassurance. Because I did mind. I had to mind. Always feeling I was being tolerated, that they never really accepted me. It was some sort of charity they were showing me. I was not one of them. I was alone. It is a special kind of loneliness, a loneliness with friends who you know do not completely accept you. You don't even accept yourself. You get anxious, over-anxious. You feel people are talking about you even if they are not. You expect them to lie, to cheat you and do you down. You are never sure if they are talking to you because they want to or because they feel they ought to. You get over sensitive. My fear was that these feelings would overpower me. Perhaps all immigrants go through this feeling of being inferior because people make them feel so. With some it leads to delinquency. Maybe it's a way of compensation, to do something bad and to feel important. We get into trouble, we get into fights because of the rage that makes us prisoner. We have to break out. It is one way out but it is temporary and doesn't lead anywhere.

You can also say to yourself, I'm better than they are. What they say won't touch me. You can kid yourself you are on top. You emphasise your education and make yourself above those that belittle you. It works with some people. They think before doing you down. But it doesn't get far with the genuine people that you really want to feel are your friends.

The sensitivity you develop in the bad times stands you in good stead when you find the genuine people and begin to learn their ways. But it depends on how much you accept yourself as you are, how genuine you can be with yourself. If you try too hard you are pushed back; if you go too slow you are left behind. Most of all, you have to believe it can be done, to believe in yourself and in the goodwill of people who mean well towards you. I could always sense how people felt about me. The genuine people stand by you, fight with you. But the others will not accept you because they fear you. And their fears are

strongly built, founded on their own insecurity. They are
threatened by the outsider who may reap some of the things
they are trying for and cannot get. It is we, the outsiders, the
immigrants, who have to understand this. Then we can tolerate
it. We may even change it. Sooner or later these very same
people will turn round and say: 'You're so different from what
I thought'. If an Englishman can say this to one immigrant, and
many have said it to me, he can say it to another, and another.
This is how integration will come about. You are on the same
wavelength and you belong to each other. But all this happens
only because you believe it can and because you are the one
who makes it happen. Then you can go forward and seek help
when you need it, ask questions, explain yourself, be
understood. I had to accept ways which were foreign to me,
ways of talking, behaving, responding, and there was never
enough time to make it easy. I had to conform. I wasn't free any
more, but I was as peace.

Eight

Demobbed

It wasn't until late November, 1947, that I left the RAF and went into the civilian hospital service. I remembered the recruiting officer in Jamaica had asked me what work I had done. I had told him I had never had a job yet but I was training in chemistry. He had said: 'You'll have to go into the MI room then. That's medical. It's nearest your work'. And that's how I came to be a medical orderly in the RAF. After the war the Colonial Office arranged for a certain number of Jamaican ex-servicemen who had been training for something before to be given grants for further education, but they stipulated it had to be in a similar field to the job done in the services. A few of us were selected and were sent off on different courses. If you were a mechanic you could take a course in mechanical engineering; if you were an electrician it would be in electrical engineering. And if you were in any way connected with medicine you were sent to train as a nurse. I had no chance to make my own decision, even the hospital was chosen for me, and I was told about it a week before I was due to report there - it was a general hospital in West London.

Up to now my knowledge of England was service life, except for the odd glimpses I had experienced whilst on leave and then my impressions were not very positive. But the blue uniform had given some protection and there were always other fellows about in camp and outside to help you out. Now I was going alone into this still strange country, much stranger than I had first thought it would be. I didn't really want to leave the RAF, yet I was excited at the thought of change. This would be a real test of the control I had been trying to build-up during those years. I had learned so much, felt so much older than my age. And I knew there would be so much more to learn. I was coming into a new society where I knew I would not be accepted at once. But I believed I now knew how to handle it.

I remember two days before coming out of the RAF, standing on a beach where it was raining and blowing and I recalled another time I had stood on a beach wishing the sea would dry up so I could walk home. I was afraid to go forward. Yet I wanted to get on, to be trained in something. I wanted to be able to go home and tell them: 'They did something good to me. I achieved something'. I wanted to show them I had come through the time, that I was older and better. The night before I left I did not sleep. I walked around the camp and when I finally went to bed I lay there thinking. Suppose they said 'black bastard'. Suppose they said why didn't I go back home to my own country. What did civilians know about us Jamaicans? Only what they read in the papers. I remembered the headlines. 'They Are British. They Came To Fight With Us'. All the incidents about us were reported. 'Jamaicans Strikes Again'. We had all kinds of trouble but the newspapers criticised prejudice and exposed it. We loved the newspapers. We used to buy them all. We knew more about the coloured troops in Leeds, in Cardiff, in Manchester, in London, than about how the war was going. These were the places where there were always fights between the West Indians and the American troops. And the newspapers always took our side. We were proud to be in a country where the papers didn't just talk about democracy and justice, they were part of these processes. But did the civilians take any notice? Did they read the papers like we did? And what did they think about it? What would they be like at the hospital? Would they keep me out? Would they put me to work by myself? Or only with other West Indians? Would they believe that I would make trouble because I was black. If I was black how could I mix with them? I was different.

I found another Jamaican was going to the same hospital and we arranged to travel down together after spending the night in Manchester.

Manchester was my kind of town. I was seeing it for the last time before going south. Nothing good had happened to me in London so far. But Manchester felt like home. It was like Jamaica to me, the only place I felt really happy. The people were friendly and cheerful and they seemed used to coloured people. I liked the North and Manchester was the centre. Colour did not seem to be such an issue here. The only discussion about it had been with some students when I was on a course in Manchester. I remember some of us being invited by an Englishwoman to her house where we met two politically minded men. They were talking about the problems of race and colour and she suddenly turned to us and said: 'You're no different from the rest of us. No different at all. You're just as good and just as bad. Unless you believe this and accept it you'll go round thinking you are different and you'll be treated different'. When we left she said: 'Remember what I said. You'll need it to keep going. It's the only way to live in this country'.

I remembered her words. They served their purpose many times.

There were other towns in the North where the people made me feel good. Once in Blackburn I wanted to see a friend and couldn't find his house. I was walking down this long street and it was raining hard. It had been raining all day. A woman from a house across the street called out: 'What do you think you're doing, walking in this rain without a coat? Come inside at once and dry your clothes! You'll catch your death of cold!' And she ran across and pulled me inside. She didn't ask any questions. I started to apologise. I couldn't protest. I said I was just looking for an address. 'Doesn't matter about that now! Go up and take off those wet things and put these on'. She put some dry clothes and a big warm dressing gown in my hands and I went upstairs and took off my uniform, heavy and soaking wet, dried myself and put on the dry clothes. I came downstairs. There was a huge coal fire burning in the living room. She hung my clothes in front of the fire and she talked to me. I explained again I'd come looking for this address and couldn't find the house. She was able to tell me the people I had been looking for had moved about a year ago but they were still only two streets away. I told her I hadn't heard from them for over a year but I had been passing through and thought I would look them up. She said: 'Don't worry. My husband will take you round there when he comes home'.

She made me tea and fussed over my uniform to get it dry without crumples. 'You men! Just like overgrown babies. No sense. Never have a proper coat on. Walking in all that rain'. To her I was just another man stupid enough to walk in the rain without a coat. She seemed to enjoy mothering me and I certainly needed it. Her husband came home. He accepted the strange sight of a cold wet black man sitting in his chair wearing his dressing gown as if it happened all the time. I was there over two hours talking with them and drinking hot sweet tea. Then he took me round to the house I had been looking for.

I had always found this immediate kindness in the North. What troubles I had were little pinpricks, usually from children who didn't know and wanted to find out. Further north still, in Glasgow, I never felt different from anyone else. No-one seemed to go out of their way to embarrass me. I felt accepted as just another customer in the cafes, the pubs, the dancehalls. I found people wanted to talk to me, to tell me about Scotland and the injustice they had suffered from the English. Yet they seemed happier than the people I met in the South. They talked to you. If you asked the way they were quick to answer and to help. I'd never had this feeling in the South, certainly not in London. People seemed indifferent. You had to have a lot of nerve to approach them because you felt they might rebuff you. You asked the way. 'I don't know. I'm a stranger here too'. The police were always helpful and so were the taxi-drivers, but you never got far if you depended on people in the street. Maybe all the people you asked were strangers. It's a big town, but sometimes you doubted that so many people could be strangers. They sat in the tube train and read their papers and if they brushed you and stepped on your toe they were polite and said: 'So sorry'. But you had the feeling that if you were to collapse they wouldn't even notice, they would step over you and pass on their way. Maybe I was wrong about this. But I had had no reason to think otherwise during my time there so far. As I reflect now after all these years I wonder whether London really can be so indifferent as it appeared to me then, because it was in London that I was eventually to settle. Back in 1947, on my last Saturday in Manchester, it was the last thing I expected to do.

We had a great night and stayed as long as we could on the Sunday. And then we took the train south. It was very late when we got to the hospital. I was still in uniform. The only civilian clothing I had was a demob suit which didn't fit. So I'd decided to wear my uniform until I could get to a good shop and choose my own clothes. I remember going into the staff dining room. Everyone stopped talking and looked up. They told me later it was the uniform that surprised them.

The next morning we saw the matron. She told us about the training. I didn't really want to be a nurse and I told her so. She was a pleasant woman, who seemed to have a mission in life to make people feel welcome. She could sense my misgivings. She said: 'Your authorities have asked me to help you and I'm going to try. But it's up to you to help me do that because it's not as bad as you think. I know you men. In the army you don't mind nursing but in civilian life it feels different. You feel it isn't a man's job. Well, it is. And you'll do well here. I know it'.

I took her word for it. I didn't have much difficulty with the work but I didn't like it much. The only troubles I had were with the other nurses, not because I was black but because I was a man. Male nurses were rare then and not popular. The sisters were very prejudiced against them. But in all the four years I spent in that hospital I never came across deep-seated colour prejudice of any kind from the staff or the patients. I was proud and surprised to find this. I felt accepted, but I never really took to the work. It took me a long time to settle and there were many talks with the matron. She was always kind. She would say she had her job to do and I had mine. I had been sent by my government and it was in my interest. I still don't know why I accepted the contract. I wondered, should I just pack up and go home? I wanted to go home so much. But, no, I didn't think I should yet. There was so much I had to learn. I ought to give myself a longer chance. So I settled into it. I was keen to learn. I had to pass those exams. I had to prove I could do it. So I studied hard and I sat the exams and I passed.

Soon after I left that hospital, I began training in psychiatry and this led eventually and, as it now seems, inevitably, to social work. But I think I began social work much earlier. The first years in England, learning to understand, to control the immediate feeling, to adapt, to tolerate, to help in times of stress, all this seems to have started me on this road. My adventures in the RAF were temporary and happened through brief chance encounters. The four year period at the hospital was the longest time I had ever spent anywhere in one place. And I got to know some of the people very well.

After about a year living in the hospital one of the staff offered me board and lodging in her house. She said that people would probably stare and make remarks about her having a coloured lodger but she said: 'I don't care. I accept you and as long as you are happy in my house you are welcome to stay. She told people I was her adopted son. She wrote to my mother and they began to correspond regularly. She was a widow with three children to bring up and I became an older brother for them. I lived there for three years. It was the first time I had ever lived in an English house. I was free from the sergeants and corporals, the rules and communal living, the insults and rejections. I was a free man. Even her son who was about seventeen called me 'brother'. We had long talks about everything that puzzled him, girls, his work, his education and his future. When I had to leave to take up psychiatric nursing at the other end of London she gave me a front door key and said: 'Whenever you are this way you can always come in and stay as long as you like. You don't have to let me know. Just come'.

I felt trusted. I belonged. I shall always remember this time and this good lady who made me her son after all the years away from my own family. My mother wrote to say how happy she was. I did the garden and cut the hedge and did all the traditionally male work about the house. People in the street used to stare at me at first but within a year they were inviting me in. My whole idea of Southerners changed. I found that given time they could be just as warm and understanding as Northerners.

I remember a patient, an old man with severe bronchial disease who had to have a hole made in his throat, a tracheotomy, to be kept alive. I was put to nurse him at night and had to keep the artificial airway open and clean. We couldn't talk much but he became so dependent and attached to me that when he was well he invited me to his house. I met his wife and their children, who were grown-up, and two little adopted girls. I spent many evenings with them and kept in touch for years.

And when this good old man died his wife wrote and asked me to come. She was on her own now. I often called and we would talk about the old days. She told me all about life in England when she was a girl, about how she met her husband and their subsequent life together. Once she called me over urgently. One of her adopted daughters, now eighteen, had run away and she had lost her. Instead of telling her own children she asked me to come. She felt a failure, she hadn't known how to bring up children right. She wanted to go down to the West End and look for her girl. I went with her. We walked through the streets asking at all the cafes and night clubs but no one knew her. Then the old lady remembered a street in Chelsea the girl had mentioned once. We went there and found the house where a woman told us the girl had gone to France with a company of dancers. The old lady was stunned. We walked sadly all the way back to her house. She didn't want to take a bus, wouldn't even take a taxi. She just wanted to walk off the blow. She never heard from the girl again. But she always had her in her thoughts. The week before she died she wrote to me and said she had made sure the girl would get her share from the will.

It remains a sad memory for me. There was nothing I could do but to be there when she asked, to listen and try to help as far as I could. You can never take over someone else's troubles. But I was grateful to her for believing I could help.

Nine

This Job Is Mine

It was in psychiatric nursing that I first discovered my 'differentness' could be an advantage. I enjoyed working especially with disturbed adolescents in a unit in my training hospital. The unit had nearly thirty staff members, doctors, nurses, psychologists and various therapists, and the young patients would try us all out to find the one with whom they felt most secure. We didn't try to please or placate or dictate to them. One boy I shall always remember. We knew he had the greatest difficulty in believing anyone or accepting any kind of help. He wouldn't eat, wouldn't sleep, wouldn't go to bed at night. He would scream and rage at us and hit out at everybody when food was mentioned. He tried and rejected all of us in turn.

Gradually I felt he was changing towards me. He took to hanging around whenever I was on duty, not obviously, but I felt he was keeping watch. The first time he showed any real movement was when he took a bite from an apple and came up to me and put the piece into my mouth. I ate it and waited. This was our first real contact, the first time he taken any initiative that called for a response from the staff. His doctor asked me to take responsibility for him, and especially to see that he took food. I don't know why the boy chose me, but I believe it was because I was different from the rest. He was different from the rest of his group too. I was the only coloured member of staff at that time. He was the only patient who would never talk to the staff and had no friends among the patients. He could identify

43

with me. And this was the beginning of his treatment. It turned out to be months of a continuous relationship. I was always with him, we went out driving, to the pictures, for walks. I always had to sit with him at table and share his food before he would eat. He trusted me. He needed support, acceptance for what he was, without question yet with understanding, to feel that he belonged - all the things I had needed. Perhaps he sensed this. Certainly I felt I could understand what he was asking for because I had sought it too and I had not known how to ask and was quick to rage because of it. He did well in his treatment and left the unit after nine months to return to his parents.

Soon after finishing psychiatric training, I felt I needed a change and, perhaps, another challenge. I enjoyed psychiatric work and made many good friends, but hospital life is protected and I decided to try my luck outside. I wanted to find out about the working man, the English working man I had heard so much about. So I applied for a job with the GPO engineering section. There was no difficulty, I was told to start the next Monday in the stores. I remember entering the stores for the first time feeling very new and unsure in my unfamiliar brown overalls. Three other fellows worked there besides me. I decided the first thing to do was to get on with the storekeeper. He took to me from the start. Whether he really accepted me in his mind or not I don't know and it wasn't important. I was a member of his staff and he seemed prepared to help me. This was important. I was there for six weeks and he promoted me. I had my own desk and my own order book and took my own orders for the stores. That was important. But I began to get worried. I couldn't understand the other three fellows. It wasn't because I was promoted. It was a kind of friendly sarcasm they had which was quite new to me. One of them started it He never used my name. It was always: 'Hello Sambo!' At first I didn't even notice but he kept on. Every morning, 'Hello Sambo'. The other two and the men coming to collect the stores took it up. I felt my name had been removed. I was Sambo. We would talk about cricket and the West Indies team but all the time the jokes were 'coloured'. I told myself I was getting too touchy. Wasn't it just the English sense of humour to use your colour to express friendship, to give you a nickname as an identity? 'Midnight' they would call out at me. 'You're looking real browned off today mate!' Always something about my colour and I never knew how to reply. I took it because I felt it wasn't malicious. But then it spread to the canteen, the billiards room, the washroom. 'Do you miss being in the jungle now. Wouldn't be so cold as it is here. What would it be like in Jamaica now? What would you be wearing eh?' My colour and my country were something to laugh about.

They talked about their women, or the ones they wished they had, the football pools, racing, all the things men talk about. But whenever they included me in the conversation there was always some reminder that I was black, different, inferior, the jungle was my place. They seemed to be trying to make me feel I owed them something, some sort of thank-you for letting me be with them, for the privilege of working with them. I couldn't make a mistake. Everything I did was commented on, jokingly at first but then it became: 'What the bloody hell are you playing at? I ordered this that and the other and you haven't got it ready yet!' I talked to the storekeeper about it but he said not to take any notice, it was just the way they were, they didn't mean any harm.

I stuck it for twelve months. It was a little education all by itself. I had been in the country nearly ten years now and thought I'd overcome most of the difficulties. They showed me I had not. It was very subtle and I couldn't handle it. I still had a long way to go.

Luckily I always had my nursing training to fall back on. I could always go and work with people who didn't play this game, perhaps had no time for it. But I didn't go back as a failure. I had learned something. And I returned to hospital work and to the security of being closer and equal with the people around me, no longer a student but a trained nurse. I could move around to gain more experience and I found jobs in many hospitals in and around London. I began to find some colour prejudice in hospital life too, though not nearly on the scale that I found outside.

In one hospital I found I was one of the best qualified male nurses there, but I became the most junior staff nurse on the wards. The promotion system was slow and seemed to depend on anything but merit, qualifications and experience. Each ward had a senior charge nurse, a deputy and then staff nurses in six grades and a few untrained nurses or students. I liked the work, it was demanding but it was the kind of personal demand that I enjoyed. However, I soon discovered that all the nursing staff were disgruntled. People waited years for promotion. If the one above you moved out, usually through reaching retirement age, you moved up one place, the nurse below you moved up to your place and so on. There was tremendous jockeying for position, just so that you could boast you were a no. 4 instead of a no. 5. I found myself joining this tortoise race with everyone else. Six months after I had been in the same ward, the no. 5 left and I expected to take his place. But I didn't. Another male nurse from another ward was moved to become no. 5. I stayed at no. 6. I didn't say anything. The next year the no. 4. left the hospital and the no. 5. took his place. I expected to be moved up this time, but I wasn't. So I started to ask questions.

The chief nurse told me it was because I hadn't been long enough in the hospital, others were waiting before me. I didn't understand this and neither did my colleagues. I was now the most experienced nurse with the highest qualifications in that ward. This pattern went on to repeat itself several times. Again I asked questions. This time I was moved to another ward where I was no. 4, but as there were only four staff nurses anyway I was still the junior one. I stood it for a while and then got angry. I went to the chief again. He tried to pacify me. Then he said I had a suspicious mind and I should go to church, it was something I had inside me.

I went back to the ward. Not long after I was refused promotion again. This time the chief said he had no choice. Did I realise how difficult it was for him? There were so many people waiting for promotion and so few places. 'Nothing against you personally, Ferron. I've had good reports from the wards about your work. It's nothing to do with your ability'. My turn would come, he said. So I waited. Two years!

Once the chief said I needed a holiday, I was becoming too

'involved'. So I took a holiday. But other people began to realise it was more than just chance or circumstance that I was being overlooked for promotion. I was one of the very few male staff nurses who was black, so they took up my case and also began to ask questions. The chief got worried. He didn't take kindly to questions. He began to check on who my friends were and some of them were also rejected for promotion. They came to be called 'Ferron's group' and were advised to keep away from me. I was a troublemaker, a monster agitator to the small group of old senior nurses around the chief. The larger group, those who worked in the wards, could see it was discrimination and they spoke up. These young English folk would not stand for injustice. They risked their own promotion prospects, their own security and the favours they might have had from the chief.

I could have left and started again somewhere else. But I had to stay and see the thing through. I would have gained nothing by leaving it unfinished. My friends stood by me, but to satisfy myself I had to depend on myself and not on their support or approval. I still believed that the best could be achieved by hard work and that justice could prevail in the end. So I worked hard, really put myself into the job. We all knew it was discrimination. But so what? We could not prove it. And even if we could it would have changed nothing. I could neither win nor lose. The system was too entrenched - even had he been so minded - for the chief himself to change it.

It was during this time that I received news from home that my mother was dangerously ill. My thoughts flew back at once to the day I left home, and then to my longing to return after the war, the years in England, all the frustrations, the days of loneliness, and the support my mother's letters had always given me. I had never again mentioned to her the peculiar life I had found here and yet she seemed to know and she comforted me. I wanted to preserve her idea of England and I did not want her to be unhappy. Now she was dangerously ill. I felt guilty. Maybe I should have told her. Maybe I should have gone home after the war. It was with these thoughts on my mind that I went to the Colonial Office and sent a cablegram to Jamaica. I sat there in a chair without moving for six hours waiting for the reply. It was bad news; her heart was failing, although everything was being done for her.

I went back to the hospital and told my story to the chief. I asked for leave to go home at once. He showed real sympathy. He said I could take as much leave as I needed and could work it off on my return. The lady who was chairman of the hospital management committee came to see me before I left. She was very kind. She wished me a safe journey and said the hospital needed me. She asked me to promise to come back. I promised. The chief gave me two months salary in advance. I needed help and understanding, and I was helped and understood. Even amidst such heights of discrimination and injustice, conscience has a way of coming forward. Humanity is stronger. I felt closer to the chief. He was a man after all.

So I left for Jamaica, sad and bewildered. The boat was slow, I hadn't been able to afford the plane. I was going home after fourteen years. There was plenty of time to think. What had I achieved? I felt a failure. My mother was on my mind all the time. What was I going to tell her?

When I arrived in Kingston my sisters were there to meet me. They tried to look pleased to see me, but I could feel their sadness as I walked down off the ship. They told me my mother was dead. Jamaica looked a strange place all of a sudden. I went through a pretence of warmth and affection but we journeyed home in silence. My only comfort was that I was home. Not until we entered the house did I really become conscious of the fact that my mother was dead. Not only dead but already buried. I was too late.

Members of my family were good, they had got over their first shock and were ready to comfort me. In the first few days of my grief I wept, I felt guilty, angry with myself, pleased to be home - yet it was not home, I felt a stranger, I belonged here yet I did not. It was where I was born and where I grew up but my mother was not here now.

Sometimes I hardly knew where I was. It was like being under hypnosis, some kind of dream. The inner control I had developed to meet the expected suspicion and rejection was with me still. Little things gave me away. My sister turned on the radio one evening very late. I told her to turn it down low, the neighbours would complain. I had learned to accept that if I was in a house I would not slam the door when I came home late, neither would I walk so that my step disturbed the sleepers next door, and my radio would be turned down low after midnight. I had forgotten I was in Jamaica now. For a whole week I had to have my bath hot, I could not get used to the idea that I could have a cold one.

My family wanted to know about England. I didn't have much to tell them. I told them a few stories about the RAF and the hospitals I had been in. They never asked about colour. In those days in Jamaica, ideas about colour were never discussed. So many people, so many colours, it was never seen as a 'problem'. They wanted to know about the England they had learned about. What is it like in London? Have you seen the Queen? Have you been in the Palace, the City, have you walked over Tower Bridge? These were the things they asked me and these were the things I told them. They didn't ask about my great disappointments so I did not tell them. I did not tell them any lies, I just didn't tell them what they didn't ask me.

Not until the end of the fourth week did I really begin to feel in touch. The hypnosis had worn off. The dream had gone. And it was time to return. It was a cloudy day when I sailed. My sisters saw me off and asked me to return soon. As I journeyed back again across the Atlantic I felt cut off from both worlds. The only reason for going back to England was my promise to the hospital that I would. I had lost my mother. I had no roots in England. Why did I want to go back? I did not know what I was hoping for, but I had hope. I was lonely. I could not look back. My link with Jamaica was cut. I could only go forward, return to England.

Soon after returning to the hospital, my feeling became stronger to fight on and fight harder. The first month was difficult. I needed friends who would understand and I was lucky to gain good support from my colleagues. The chief and his committee were kind too. He began to show more understanding of my position in the ward. Though I did not get promotion at once I received recognition and reassurance and that was my first need at this time. I was still on the same ward, still at no. 4. But I had good friends and felt I was of some use to the patients. I knew there had been injustice but I always kept hoping that things would change. And they did change. I became no. 3 quite soon and then was moved to another ward to become no. 2. I felt my effort had not been in vain.

I did not stay long in the hospital after that. When I left, there was no bitterness in me because my hopes had been fulfilled. Other coloured nurses with full qualifications were being recruited and would get better treatment because someone had made a stand. Prejudice is in all of us. It comes from fear, ignorance, insecurity, blindness and distortion, envy and threat. A mental hospital is always full of these. But I did not leave the hospital service. I got another appointment at another hospital, a therapeutic community, more in keeping with my experience and qualifications.

Life here was completely different. It was to bring me to a brighter future. People worked together in a team and judged each other not by colour or age or years of service, but only according to their ability. It was exacting work, the most difficult I had ever done. But the hospital had something new to offer. It was run democratically and people could discuss, had to discuss and examine everything that happened. Decisions were reached by consensus. It was part of the work, part of the way things were run. Everyone had not only the right but the duty to ask questions. We were not rigidly stratified into grades, we were just men and women, patients and staff, working together and everyone's contribution was valued and needed. I felt confident and could begin to develop professionally. My interest in patients' families and in social work began to grow and I was encouraged to follow it. I remember all the staff in that community. I always shall. They put me on a new road. It was a real turning point for me. I could look back, I could consolidate, come to terms with myself and my real situation, live with it and even begin to enjoy it.

Ten

The War Is Over

In my nursing career then, things were going well. Being black was now never an issue with the patients or with the nurses and doctors I worked with. I was just another nurse, quite a good one I think. The only real trouble I had had was with the nursing authorities in that one hospital, and even though it took the death of my mother for them to realise I was as vulnerable and human as anyone else, the trouble I had there led to better things. Outside the hospital and away from people who knew me, it was different.

Things began to change around 1950. The feeling between immigrants and the native English changed too. The war was over and was being forgotten. The elections came and went. The national health service began. People were rebuilding and thinking ahead. The foreign troops had gone home, including most of the West Indians. The few who stayed seemed to be absorbed into the community easily enough. There seemed to be no fear of them. There was talk about the Jews. People were shocked about what happened in Germany, searching their consciences to look for what had gone wrong and how they might have stopped it. There was a lot of talk about 'racialism', some realistic, some shaming and some merely pious. It wasn't until the later 1950s that coloured immigrants came in greater numbers and became more obvious. The talk then changed showing how shallow and false had been much of the earlier sentiment against racism. But this wasn't an immediate thing, the feeling against black immigrants grew gradually. Then over the years racism became accepted as part of the life of the country; sometimes it was obvious, sometimes hidden, but always there.

Outside hospital I was just another black immigrant, subject to all the slights and rejections from the ignorant, the unthinking and the blind. To get them to think and look again, that was the thing to do.

I gave this advice to an African friend who had decided to stand as Labour candidate in a local election. He believed that the one way to challenge the colour problem in this country was for a black man to take part in local politics. He asked me to help him, especially with his speeches. We sat down and worked on them for many nights. Then one evening he came over and told me he was fed up and was going to withdraw his name from the ballot. He said: 'I went to a hundred houses today and knocked on the doors and thirty times the door was slammed in my face. They would not even look at me. These people will never want a black man to represent them'.

I reminded him that in the beginning he had told me his belief that politics was the only way to break through. 'You knew at the start it would be hard going. If everyone opened their doors to you it would not be necessary for you to break down the barrier. You're in this because the door *is* slammed in your face. You've got to put up with it. If you want to break through you must risk rejection and meet it when it comes'.

We argued it out. He wondered if this really was the right way. Next day we both went round together. We must have gone to a hundred houses again and at every third one the door was slammed on us. I knew now what it felt like. But I advised him again to go forward. I went with him and listened to him talking, asking people to vote for him. He was good, but every night he was in turmoil. He thought he had taken on too much. He still wanted to give it up but didn't know how, it had gone too far now. He was sure he would get nowhere. But the election day came and to our amazement he was elected councillor for that area. He told me that during his first speech he felt the fulfilment of his dream. Now he could really start. I was pleased for him.

My dream was being fulfilled too, though I never aspired to fulfilment in public life as he did. I just wanted to be understood and accepted for what I was and still am. And to reach it I worked through my contact with people wherever I was and however difficult it proved, patiently and without anger. On an individual person to person level it nearly always worked. I learned a lot about people that way, the polite little tricks, the self-deceptions, the covering up and the buck passing - all to avoid facing their own fears and failings.

But sometimes it was bigger and more sinister. Sometimes it was more than the landlord who refused me entrance, the shopgirl who shuddered when she touched my money, the barman who told me to get back to the jungle, the boss who denied me deserved promotion.

I bought a car and had to take out my first insurance. The man in the agency asked my name. I told him. 'It doesn't sound quite English', he said, 'but I think it will pass'. I asked him what difference that made and he told me: 'If your name sounds foreign you'll have to pay twenty per cent more for a policy'. He tried to get me a policy but only after I had agreed to pay the extra. He assured me that whatever company I tried it would be the same. And he was right. Wherever I went it was: 'I'm sorry but you people have more accidents than people here'. When I asked why I should be penalised when I had no more accidents than anyone else, I would be told, 'It makes no difference. The policy isn't made just for you. It's made for all foreigners'. I needed the car for my job so I had to pay the extra.

The first time I decided to go to Europe for a holiday I ended up paying double insurance. I had applied for a green card some weeks before from my insurance company, and had got no reply. I checked and was told it would come. A few days before my holiday was due to begin I was told the company would not issue a green card. Because I was coloured? I checked with somebody who happened to be with the same company and he had got a green card without difficulty. So I went to see the agent. He told me of an insurance company in the city who would help me. It was a foreign company and didn't mind insuring coloured people. I had to pay them ten pounds for two weeks insurance and then I got my green card. By now I only had twelve days left, a week of my holiday had already been spent in trying to get a green card to go away!

For eight years I went on paying the extra twenty per cent. Then, one day when I went to pay my premium, the agent, a young man, took sympathy on me. He asked how long I had been in this country. I counted up. It was nearly eighteen years. He said: 'I cant see why after eighteen years you have to pay extra. After all you learned to drive here, didn't you?' I said I had.

'I'm not supposed to do this but you're a good bloke, always pay on time. My niece works for a company who I'm sure wouldn't charge extra to a coloured man if he's been in the country as long as you have. Don't tell anyone I told you this or I'll lose my job'. He gave me the address and told me to tell his niece he had sent me. 'If they give you a policy you can cancel the one you have with us and instead of paying this premium to me pay it on your new one'.

'Why do you do this for me?'

'I don't like injustice. I think its unfair. You're no different from me. You drive as well as me. I think its wrong. I'm employed here so I suppose I shall have to do as they say, but this is just between you and me'.

I went to the office where his niece was working and got my policy. And from then on I have paid the same insurance as other men in this country. Once again it showed me that some individuals will not stand for injustice even though they are supposed to carry out a discriminatory practice. I shall always remember that young man. He helped me because he knew me, that I paid up on time, and he wouldn't be a party to his firm's unjust practice.

My car enmeshed me in much legal red tape over the years. Once, after being involved in an accident, I went to see a lawyer for advice. He told me he would only take my case if he thought he could win it, he never took a case if there was the slightest chance he would lose. 'I've had thirty years practice and never lost a case', he said, 'There's no prejudice in me. I'll take a coloured man's case as readily as that of the next man but I never take a case, coloured or white, if there's a chance I might lose it'. He looked at me intently. 'I don't particularly like coloured cases. For a coloured man to win he's got to have a really good case. The moment he enters court and the jury sees him he's already lost the first round, because most of the jury will be prejudiced. They're only human and they can't consider a case without remembering that you're coloured. In a criminal case the verdict goes against you even if you didn't do it. In matrimonial actions you've got to have a very good case indeed to win against your wife, especially if she's white. It's a natural thing, isn't it? That's why I like to be honest with you.

I left his office feeling I'd already lost the case. If this had been ten years ago, I thought, I would have been in despair. I might even have turned against authority and gone bad. But by now it was no surprise. I'd come to expect it. And I accepted what he said. I realised it would be impossible for a jury to forget I was black, guilty or not. So when this lawyer told me I had already lost the first round I believed him. He brought me again face to face with this great problem of being different, the fantastic handicap of being black in a white world. He was a man of thirty years experience, he was being honest, he knew what he was talking about, but it didn't make me any happier. However, the case was tried and the verdict went in my favour. But he didn't take it. It went through the magistrates court and never reached a jury.

So many times I could have found myself on the wrong side of the law simply because people assumed that by being black I must also be bad. On holiday in Guernsey I went into a cafe and sat down at the only table with empty chairs. Two young men were also sitting there and soon a third middle-aged man joined them. They talked among themselves and I drank my coffee. With my suitcase beside me it was obvious that I had just arrived for a holiday. I paid for my coffee and left to find a hotel. I had booked but was two days later than I expected in arriving and the room had gone. As I went outside the two young men came up to me, one on my right and one on my left. I didn't know what they wanted. My first thought was that they wanted to rob me. But they didn't. They wanted to offer me money, a hundred pounds. 'How would you like to earn a hundred pounds this minute?'

'I'd have to do something pretty fantastic to do that'.

They looked around. The third man was standing now in the doorway of the cafe looking up the street, the one on my right was looking down the street, while the one on my left did the talking.

'You're going to France aren't you?'

'No. I'm staying in Guernsey'.

'What about a nice little trip to France?'

He showed me a parcel. 'This is worth a lot of money. A man will meet you off the boat over there and he'll take it. He'll meet you as you come through the customs. They won't open it'.

'How can you be sure they won't open it?'

'Because there is only a scarf and a jumper inside'.

'But why send a scarf and jumper to France?'

'My friend over there finds it very difficult to get this kind of scarf and jumper in France'.

'But why pay me a hundred pounds to take it over?'

'We had some luck today. We won some money and we just feel generous. If you do us a favour the least we can do is be decent to you about it'.

I said no thanks. The other fellow looking down the street took a step closer to me and said quietly: 'We'll put you on the boat and once you're on it you can't get off. You will have to keep going'.

'You couldn't do that', I said, 'because I should kick up such a fuss everyone would wonder what was going on'.

The third man said: 'We're wasting our time with him'.

And they suddenly walked quickly away. Why pick on me?, I wondered. But just as they left a woman came up and asked me what they had wanted. I told her. 'Don't mix with them. They smuggle things. They've got something they wanted you to smuggle across. I don't know what the police are doing. I hope they get caught this time'.

She asked me where I was staying and I told her I was looking for a room.

'I've got a guest house'. And she took me there. She ran this guest house with her husband and a son and daughter. I had a glorious time there. I was taken round the island and met many people. I was even asked to give a talk to a young people's club about Jamaica. It was my first public speech. I felt renewed. I climbed the hills, swam in the sea, lazed on the beach. When I was leaving I handed over fourteen guineas for two weeks but the woman would only take ten because I'd only stayed ten days.

Once again things had started badly and turned out well for me through a chance meeting. Some people associate black with bad, some don't even notice the black. And for some, black even means goodness.

One little incident I shall always treasure. It was during a visit to Wales to attend the wedding of two of my nursing friends. I was walking through a little village in Carmarthenshire and passed some young children on the bridge. They looked at me shyly and they followed me, walking a yard or so away. They very much wanted to speak. They were friendly curious little children. I was new, I was black, I was different. I stopped. They stopped. Then one of them came up and asked me: 'Are you the new minister?' The other said: 'You are coming to preach in our chapel on Sunday'? I was touched. Maybe the only black man they had ever seen was a minister. It was sweet and very gentle. I replied: 'No. I'm not the minister. I'm a visitor'. They smiled and looked at me. I'd never been mistaken for a minister before. I asked them about the coal tips outside the village and they told me their fathers all worked in the mines. It was pleasant talking there in the sunshine with these little Welsh children, though I couldn't understand all they were saying. I left them and went on up the hill to find my friends' house. I attended the wedding so I did go to their chapel after all. It was a pleasant occasion. I remember my visit to Wales, a peaceful, gentle country.

Eleven

That's a White House, Sir

For me it was never far down any road before I met good people. It is still like that. But people are hard to know. You have to be in a situation long enough with them before they accept you. The first difficulty is to get into the right situation, then you have to stay with it, persist and try all ways until you and they develop an understanding.

When I had just started work in a hospital in Surrey, I applied by telephone for a room advertised in the local paper, a front room on the first floor at two pounds ten shillings a week, which was as much as I could afford at the time. The lady asked me to come round and see it that evening after I had finished duty. I went round and knocked on the door. She opened it, looked a little taken aback and said: 'Oh! Was it you on the phone?'

'Yes', I said.

'You're sure it was you? You sounded so different on the phone. I didn't know it would be you'.

'Who did you expect it would be?'

She flustered. 'Well, I don't know really. I thought it would be a white man I suppose. It sounded like it on the phone'.

I didn't respond but asked to see the room. 'Just a minute,' and she shut the door. She could at least have left it open I thought. I also had a feeling I wasn't going to get the room. She was back in a few minutes.

'I'm so very sorry but my husband phoned just this minute and told me he has offered the room to a friend at work'. She was sorry I had wasted my time coming all this way but she

58

hoped I would understand.

I said: 'If you'd known I was black would you have asked me to come?'

'Well, to tell you the honest truth, no, I wouldn't'.

'Why not?'

'It's very difficult round here. I personally have nothing against coloured people but people round here are a funny lot. I believe there's black and white in all of us but people round here don't see it like that. I couldn't risk it'.

'What is there to risk?'

'It's not because of what they think. But you must understand how difficult it would be for me. No one would speak to me. I'd go into a shop and no-one would speak'.

'Is it really as bad as that now?'

'Yes', she said, and she seemed to be apologising.

'But surely you can stand up to what people say. You're your own boss in your own house'.

'And you're a very good talker', she said, 'What is your language? Where do you come from? You speak English very well'.

I told her. 'I see. I thought you must have learned to speak English when you came here. I'm so very sorry about all this'.

She seemed a good woman and she was beginning to listen. I decided to risk it.

'Since I've been talking to you I've got the impression you are a kindly honest woman, yet you began by hiding something'.

'I'm not hiding anything'.

'You know your husband didn't telephone. You knew when you opened the door that no-one else had taken the room. You knew you'd decided you wouldn't let it to a black man. Why couldn't you be honest with me?'

She thought for a minute, then she said: 'Would you like a cup of tea?' I said I would and she invited me inside.

'It seems so awful really. Of course, my husband didn't telephone. I feel terrible about it. I've read about people rejecting coloured people and I never thought I'd do the same thing. But it's the neighbours. And my husband is very strict about who he has in the house'.

I said nothing.

'What about in Jamaica? Do you get on with the white people there?'

'Yes I do. There's no difference. But we don't seem to let rooms in Jamaica. Everyone has their own house'.

'What about in the towns?'

'Perhaps. I don't know. I've always lived in the country'.

We talked on. I felt that there was a woman for the first time trying to be honest about her colour prejudice. She was talking to a black man face-to-face and finding out that he was a human being who felt deeply about being rejected but who could take it, and discuss it. She didn't know what to do.

'You might like to see the room now you are here'.

It was just as she had described it over the telephone, a big room, well furnished and warm. 'I provide meals because there's only one kitchen'. We went back downstairs. She told me about her husband and her little boy who had just done well in his exams at school. And the time passed pleasantly. 'I could talk to my husband when he comes home. He might let you have the room'.

But I didn't want the room now. I had felt insulted but I was pleased. I'd done my job. She would remember meeting a black man, finding he could talk English and wasn't a monster.

It is not only the ignorant and the unthinking who are prejudiced. Sometimes it is the very people who have been victims of prejudice themselves. I went to see a flat in Fulham. The landlord was German. He told me he didn't like foreigners! 'Nothing against you personally but I don't take coloured tenants. The white tenants don't like it'.

'Have you ever asked them?'

'No. I just believe so'.

'Maybe it's easier for you to say it's the white tenants'.

'Look! I don't argue with you. I just tell you'.

'But I want to understand why you have to pretend. If you've never had coloured people in your house you can't know anything about them'.

'No. That's true, but I don't want to find out either'.

That was more to the point. But I couldn't leave it there.

'Surely you've been turned away yourself'.

'How do you know that?'

'I can tell by your accent you're not from this country. You've gone through humiliation yourself'.

'Yes', he said, 'I come from Germany. I thought I was German but I didn't like what was going on there so I went to Poland, then the Germans came to Poland and I escaped to England. I have nothing to do with what happened in Germany. I was not a party to it. Anyway it's got nothing to do with this'.

'It's got everything to do with it. You are a foreigner in a strange country. You know what it's like to be turned away. Yet you're doing the same thing to me. You have this big house. You want tenants, quiet tenants who will keep things tidy and pay their rent. Yet you turn me away because I'm black. How do you know your white tenants will keep things tidy and pay the rent?'

'I don't know. I just have to risk it'.

'So you turned down coloured people because they're not white. You know nothing about us. You don't even want to know'.

'You should take up law', he said.

'Laws are for criminals. This isn't a crime, it's injustice. If you knew about law you'd know the difference. You might understand what I'm trying to say. I don't really want the room now, but I do want you to understand'.

He said nothing, so I went on.

'You can understand better than most because you've suffered the same, but you're white. People don't know you're different until you open your mouth, but they can see I'm different at a glance. I don't even get the first chance. Can't you see how much more difficult it is for us? And it's people like you who have known suffering and rejection who could help us'.

'I should like you to come inside and have a drink', he said. I went inside and we talked. 'It's only when you discuss these things you see how stupid you really are', he said. He pointed to some black boys playing in the street. 'I've never spoken to them. Never thought they were very bright anyway'. Then he said: 'I've never refused a room to a coloured man, because I've never had one come for a room before. But some of these English are very funny people. I can't afford not to keep in with them. And I've had American tenants here who talk about niggers. They have money and if I had black men here they wouldn't come. I'm in business. I have to attract the best customers. But you make your point well. Tell you what, there's a man upstairs leaving at the end of the month. I want someone I can trust, wouldn't mind letting you have it if you like'. He opened his arms and held his hands out and looked to heaven. 'Who am I to turn away a coloured man?'

He showed me the room. It was very nice but he wanted four pounds for it. That was too much for me. I was still only getting a staff nurse's salary at the time. I thanked him but turned it down.

'Not at all', he said, 'and whenever you're passing by and looking for a room when your money gets better don't forget to call in and contact me. I like you. You've opened my eyes. Do all the coloured people talk like you?'

I told him I didn't know but if he talked to some he might find out. We parted on good terms. You really had to work hard to get somewhere to live, I found. And when you'd got your point across you often felt you couldn't take the place anyway. But sometimes I was lucky. I lived for five years in houses owned by one woman who was a very good landlady. My luck came in answer to a scribbled little advertisement on a board outside a sweetshop. I decided to try my chances. She welcomed me into her house. She said she liked having West Indian tenants. She had houses in different parts of London and I could get a room in any of them any time I wanted.

She gave me a big ground floor room at the back of the house and I took to doing the garden and fixing the fence. She appreciated this. The other tenants never bothered about the garden. I'd been there about two years and found I had become a sort of senior tenant in the house. She came to me one day and said: 'I trust you and I want to prove it'.

'Why do you have to prove it?' I said.

'What I really want is to ask you to help me out. I have four houses in this district and it's a long way for me to come every week to collect the rents. Could you do it for me? You could bring the money to my house each week, and I'd take twenty five per cent off your rent'.

I thought this was a very reasonable idea. The English tenants told me I should get my rent free not just reduced but I didn't want that. I wanted to keep my independence. So I began to collect the rents each week for her. What I hadn't bargained for was everyone coming to me for light bulbs, to fix the fuses, to complain about the pipes being blocked. I became a sort of caretaker as well. There was one time a white tenant refused to give me his rent. He didn't see why he should. I didn't press him but the landlady came up and told him that was the arrangement and if he didn't like it he could move out. So I used to find his rent outside my door every Saturday morning. He would never give it to me directly. He never got on with the other tenants and quite soon he moved out anyway. The demands for me to fix things eventually became too much. I never seemed to get any time to myself. So I asked the landlady to relieve me of the responsibility. She understood and did so. She was a good woman and she trusted me. I became a friend of the family and when I left after five years I found I had new confidence. Whenever I was looking for rooms in other areas I would remember her and could knock on other doors without worrying about the inevitable first rejection.

I believed that to integrate myself, really to live among the people around me, I was the one who would have to make the first effort and work through the first rejection. I couldn't do this if I just gave up and lived only among my own kind though I knew they would never reject me. If I went to a Jamaican landlord and he had a room I knew he would always let me have it. But that would mean I was avoiding my struggle and turning back from my goal. I would meet English people only at work and that was not my idea at all. Without this goal to work towards I would have reached despair like so many others.

Finding somewhere to live was a problem for every immigrant especially the new one who had not yet learned the ways of the English. He would see a house advertised at a reasonable price. Often he did not get told that the property was due for demolition, that it was requisitioned, or was only on a short lease. He often did not understand these things. He believed that when he bought a house it was his. Then he found out it was not his at all. A friend of mine bought a house of four rooms for £1500. He thought he had a bargain. I asked him if he was sure he had read the papers carefully, especially the small print. Was he sure he had not been caught? But he had read all the documents and all the small print and it was genuine, he said, and he had paid cash for it. He lived there happily with his young family for seven years, then came a letter offering him the sale of the lease. He couldn't understand it. A solicitor told him the house had been on a seven year lease and that unless he bought the lease the house would no longer be his. He was astounded. He could never really understand what it was all about. Fortunately he could afford the extra £1000 for the lease and he bought it. I'm sure he did the right thing, it would have been worse for him if he had been turned out.

Many immigrants have been caught like this. They cannot afford to buy the lease and fall back on renting a house, or more likely a room. Then they find themselves caught in a different way, even by their own countrymen.

Some Jamaicans I know suddenly changed when they came to this country and became landlords themselves. They charged rents just as high as any English landlord, and they threatened immigrant tenants that if they went to an English landlord he would charge them even more. They put the new immigrant in a desperate position. He knew he would have to struggle to be accepted by an English landlord so he would give up and pay a high rent in his own countryman's house where he knew he would not be rejected. The Jamaican landlord soon found he could get more money by renting each room separately instead of making them into flats. He might get more people in that way but the house could quickly turn into a slum. A married couple, for example, would start life in one room. Then children arrived and they needed a second room, and then a third. So they would take separate rooms in the same house and pay more than if they had a three roomed flat - the landlord making a bigger profit. So desperate were young married couples that they took whatever they could get. The Jamaican landlord did not turn them out like the English landlord just because they had children. And he would not turn the young single fellow or girl away just because they were black. He made no conditions and no restrictions. They could have parties, cook curries, have children, and have visitors and lodgers. He didn't mind. He allowed free use but equally he often didn't bother about the upkeep of the house by letting repairs go and buying cheap shoddy furniture. If tenants complained he was quick to point to others waiting for the rooms.

New Jamaican immigrants were astonished that their own people could be so cold and mean, that they could do to their fellow countrymen just what they accused some English landlords of doing. Many people have told me that they would never have believed their own countrymen could change so.

Thus, from prejudice, desperation and the exploitation of the weak by the strong, a house is classified as a slum. Native English and immigrants are both involved in making it so. And because the poorer, newer, less established group live in poorer housing, everyone else believes it is because they want to, that they turn good houses into slums 'because they like it that way'. New immigrants trying to settle in a house are amazed when they see English tenants moving out. Other black immigrants move in and the house becomes a 'black house'.

When different groups live without contact they grow apart. The only things they have in common are suspicions and misbeliefs about each other. A wrong develops to the point where it is accepted as normal. And children grow up knowing no other way.

I was visiting a patient's house in Brixton one day. As I went up to the door to ring the bell two black children playing in the street stopped their game and ran up shouting nervously: 'That's a white house, sir. There's a white woman living there. It's not a coloured house'.

I felt suddenly sad. These children, so young, were growing up in a street of black and white houses, where English and West Indians lived separate lives. Already they had accepted the separateness. They were warning me to keep away from the white house. They had learned from their parents that a black man does not go into a white house. It was very sad and worrying.

Twelve

The Let-Down

A friend in Jamaica wrote to me that his brother had been over in England a year and his family had only heard from him once. He gave me his address and asked me to find out if he was still there and to tell him to write home. On one of my days off from work I looked up the address but the people told me he had moved. They gave me another address in North London. The house was old and the garden neglected. The hedge had not been cut for a long time and the gate was held together with string. I untied the string and went up the path and rang the bell. An untidy woman of about fifty came to the door.

'You again,' she said. I was stunned for a moment. I'd never seen her before.

'You've been here this morning before haven't you?'

I said I'd never been to the house before and told her the name of the man I was looking for.

'You all look the same to me. I can't keep track of all the names. Do you mean the one on the first floor? If it is him he won't be here much longer I can tell you. I'm not putting up with him and his friends. Sly they are, and he's a real nuisance. I think he's a bit phoney, don't you?'

I told her I didn't know the man.

'Well, there's another one on the top floor. He's a weird one too. Don't understand him at all. Never says much and he's always up there. Never leaves his room'.

I asked if I could go up and see if he was the man I was looking for.

'Wait. I'll see what name he gives. Not that that's anything to go by. I never take their names seriously. They give one on one day and another the next. One of you Nigerians gave me a name I couldn't even spell. Then his wife came looking for him and she gave me a different name altogether'.

As it turned out the man on the top floor had given the name I had in the letter. She let me inside and I went upstairs to the third floor and knocked on the door. The stairs and the landing hadn't seen a brush for months. The door opened and I introduced myself to a tall thin fellow and told him why I had come.

'I don't know you', he said.

'No, but your family asked me to find you. Your brother knows my family and he wrote and asked me to come and see why you hadn't written home'.

'I couldn't write home. I've got nothing to tell them. What could I tell them?'

He waved an arm around the room. It had a bed but no mattress. One blanket was spread across the springs and the others were in a heap on the floor beside a bowl with dirty water and a jug. There was one chair with a cushion missing, but no table and no wardrobe. His clothes hung on a peg on the wall. 'Is this all you have?' I asked, 'Why haven't you at least got a mattress?'

'That's what I keep telling the woman. I couldn't write to my parents about it, could I? When I came here I asked for a mattress. The woman said a Nigerian boy had been here before and he burned it so she decided she would not buy any more. She says if anyone wants a mattress they must buy their own. But I can't. I intended to buy one but I never got around to saving the money'.

'What did you do in Jamaica?', I asked him.

'I grew up there but when I was eighteen I went to America with my uncle. I took a degree in engineering and then I went back home and got a job on the railway. I was doing quite well but then the fever to come to England got me and I thought I could do better over here. I went to the Labour Exchange when I got here, but they said they didn't have anything for anyone with my qualifications. So I started looking in the papers for a job myself. I saw plenty going but whenever I went for an interview they always told me I hadn't got enough experience. So then I got a job on the buses but it wasn't my kind of work. Then I got a job in a factory greasing rivets and cleaning machinery. It's a good job, well paid'.

'Yes, but it isn't engineering'.

'I know that. But if you're a West Indian you can't get that sort of job here'.

'How much do you make a week?'

'Nearly eighteen pounds. They let me do overtime. I only started two weeks ago. I'm saving to go home. That's why I'm living like this. I still owe money I borrowed for my fare here. I have to pay that back first. Then I thought I'd write home and send some money to my mother. If you write to my brother tell him I'll be writing soon, but don't tell him anything else'.

Then he stopped speaking and lay down on the bed and turned away from me and wept. 'Don't you have any friends?', I asked him.

'Man, you can't have friends round here. I don't want that kind. These boys get up to all sorts of tricks. I go to evening classes. I'm doing a course in commerce. There's a cousin I visit sometimes. But apart from that I never see anyone. I don't like London. I don't want to know any of the people I've met here'.

I left him and went home. I felt for him. I knew his suffering. And I knew he was working it out for himself, working out where he went wrong, why he had come, how much better his life would have been in Jamaica, if only he'd known what it would be like here. This was what was going on in his mind. But I knew he would survive. His goal would save him. He could so easily have gone the other way, become angry and want to destroy his life or get into trouble. But he wouldn't. He would suffer inwardly and alone. How many suffered like him? They had a bit of paper with their qualifications but nothing to back it up. The paper didn't matter. The colour didn't. The paper and an influential friend might help, but the paper by itself was nothing.

There was a qualified electrician I knew in Norwood. He had trained in Jamaica where he had a good job but he came here for further training. He intended to go to evening classes but the only job he could get would not release him. He was a porter in a hospital, who worked awkward hours. He mostly spent his time washing dishes. He couldn't leave the job until he found something better. But he hadn't given up. He was still out to better himself.

I met another like him in a friend's house in Balham. He'd been a policeman in Jamaica but he left the Force to come to England because he thought he could make a better living here. He knew he would never get into the Police Force here and now he worked as a roadsweeper. The pay was better than in the Jamaican Police and that's why he did it. But his main aim was to get back home again.

When he left for work in the morning, he told me, he wore his best suit and changed into overalls when he got there and he always wore a hat pulled well over his eyes so that no-one would recognise him. When he finished work he would change back into his best suit to travel home in the bus. He never told his friends what his job was. He never told his family, wouldn't dare let them know. He sent money home regularly and always told them he was doing very well. His wife wanted to join him but he always put her off. She mustn't know how it really was.

When I met him he had come to terms with his situation. He accepted degradation, took the only job he could find and arranged things so that he kept his self worth, like changing his clothes so that no-one would know. He would survive because he had a goal. He was going home.

Another friend came to this country already a qualified and experienced mechanic. He tried for many jobs but was always turned away. Finally he got a job on the buses, but he was always looking for a mechanics job. Once he heard of one going in a garage but when he turned up they told him they wanted a driver. Then he got a mechanic's job but the firm was taken over and he was made redundant. He got depressed. He had tried for so long and when he finally got the job for which he was trained he lost it.

He was married with two children. His wife pressed him to go to the National Assistance office but he was too proud. She insisted it wasn't charity and that the children must eat. He decided to write to his parents for money to tide him over, but he would not apply for National Assistance. Finally his wife went and got some money from them. He was blazing angry and they had tremendous rows which nearly broke up the marriage. He didn't want charity. He would rather starve. His wife turned on him. Would he starve the children too? In time, the money came from Jamaica and soon after that he got another mechanic's job.

This is the kind of story that never gets told. All we heard at the time were stories about immigrants hanging round the National Assistance expecting money for nothing. Yet most West Indians I know are proud people. They want to earn a living not beg it. They do not want the world to know their troubles and, most of all, they don't want the people at home to know. And because of their pride the whole thing gets worse. The hardest thing is to bear the slights and rejections on your own. You can never tell them at home how it really is. You just tell them the good things and you say to yourself you cannot hurt them and anyway they wouldn't understand. So more new immigrants had come over believing, just as I had done, that England was the mother, that here would always be the welcome, the love, the chance to grow and find the good life, just as we were always taught at school. Then the let-down came, which was difficult to survive without a strong personal goal in view. There were, and are, plenty of good people in England but you did not find them by huddling together in tight little groups, you did not find them by going against their ways and their laws, you did not find them by locking yourself in your room and only talking to your black neighbour. You only found them if you accepted yourself as an individual and were prepared to go forward from your room and your house into the community, into the street, with your head high, to talk to people, to work with them and help them to develop a confidence in you, to tackle them as an intelligent man, to face them even at the height of prejudice, to mix freely with confidence and risk being rejected and insulted, then and then only do you begin to meet the good people.

Thirteen

My Jamaican Identity

A Nigerian friend of mine invited me to a party at his house. I wondered what it would be like at an African party. I went and found about twenty people there. I was the same colour. No-one could see the difference. But I knew at once there was. They all spoke a language I did not understand. At an English party I felt black and though they might try to make me welcome, the only thing we would have in common was the language. At this African party, the only thing we had in common was our colour. It was not enough. I felt just as foreign, as unwanted, as rejected as if I were at an English party listening to insinuations about my colour. I couldn't talk to people and didn't know what they were saying. I felt they were saying they didn't want a Jamaican at their party. I told my friend. He was surprised for a moment. 'I'd forgotten you were Jamaican. Come on and I'll introduce you round'.

We joined a group of about eight people and he said: 'This is my friend Eric. He's Jamaican so speak English will you?'

They looked me up and down. The girls walked away. The boys apologised for speaking in their own language. 'It's always like this when we are together' they told me, 'We find it easier to relate in our own language and it's good to have the chance to speak it'.

I said I understood. I couldn't say more because immediately one of the boys started again in his own language and they all joined in leaving me in the middle not understanding a word.

I moved around the party, I listened, I had a drink. When I left

I wished it could have been different. Where did I belong? Should I go to my English friends' parties and put up with colour prejudice, or should I go to African parties and not understand what was said, or should I stick to Jamaican parties and not mix with a range of other people at all? It was a conflict. I supposed I would have to adjust to each and accept each as they were and hope I would gain something, some understanding that would help me to be more tolerant and not to expect that things would change *for* me. Perhaps things might be able to change *with* me.

Prejudice seems to belong to all races and all groups. Is it perhaps the worst evil in man? It is not only from black to white and white to black, white people are prejudiced against each other, and so are black people. West Indians have certain attitudes towards Africans, yet we are all of the same stock. The English have certain attitudes towards the Germans, the French, the Dutch, the Belgians, and Europeans have certain attitudes towards white Americans, yet they are all of the same stock.

I remember going to find a room in Balham. A Nigerian opened the door.

' I heard you had a room to let'.

'Yes, we have a room to let. Where are you from?'

I told him. 'Jamaica?' 'Yes'. One of his friends joined him at the door and they talked in their own language and laughed at something. So I said: 'What is the joke? Are you letting a room or not?'

'You a Jamaican coming to an African house for a room?'

And they laughed again. 'What is wrong with that?', I said. They asked me to come inside, still laughing. Two girls immediately left the room as I walked in. The two fellows showed me round the house. 'We're all Nigerians living here', the one who had opened the door said. He seemed reluctant to let me see the room. He only showed it to me, he said, because his friend had said it would be all right. Twice he reminded me that only Nigerians lived there. His attitude prompted me to ask why he had to repeat it. He said: 'When I advertised the room I wanted Africans only'.

'You didn't put that in the advertisement. All it said was

"Room to let. Coloured welcome"'.

'I don't really want Jamaicans living here', he said.

'Why not?'

'They're noisy and I don't get on with them'.

'Have you known any'?

'I've met a few but we don't really want anything to do with them'.

'What do you dislike about us?'

'What do Jamaicans dislike about Africans?'

'Maybe those who say that don't understand you'.

'You have a good point. But we prefer to stay as we are. You Jamaicans think you are so different. You don't really want to mix with us'.

'But I've just come to you for a room'.

'Oh yes, you'll take a room in an African house because there's no Jamaican house in the street with an empty room. But as soon as there is you'll move out of here quick enough'.

This was something new to me. I usually heard this sort of thing from an English landlord. I never thought I would hear it from people of my own colour. He made no further move to offer me the room. He went on complaining about Jamaicans mixing with the white people all the time, thinking they were so superior. Finally he said: 'Goodbye'. It was a dismissal. As I walked away I realised I had some new thinking to do. We black people ought to be looking into our own relations with each other. Prejudice divided us too. The Africans usually saw West Indians as pro-European. I wondered if this was driving us closer to Europeans and creating further friction with the Africans. Should we not feel guilt for turning away from our own fellow men? Were we closer to the Europeans in our lifestyle, our customs, our beliefs; our language is English, with only our black skin reminds us of our origin?

There were also big differences in the peoples of the West Indian islands too. Most of us came here full of local prejudices from home. Each island has its own customs and mixtures of culture and in our little world we felt superior to the next island. The Barbadian doesn't want to be mistaken for a Jamaican, the Trinidadian doesn't want to be thought of as a Guianese. The

Englishman may say all blacks are the same, but West Indians know how different they are.

We Jamaicans see ourselves as a proud people. In Jamaica the land is divided into small holdings and every owner feels he is the little lord of the manor. He has a strong feeling of independence even though he may be poor. He has a bit of land to grow his food and feed his children and leave to them when he dies.

Jamaicans love their children and their old people. Families are big and there is always room for one more. They used to live closely with a strong link between the generations. It was normal for the grandparents to bring up the young children of their daughters and sons. It used to be a local custom that needed no planning and no litigation. If a woman had too many children to care for herself there was nothing wrong or unusual in her sister or an aunt taking one of them to bring up as her own. It didn't need legal papers, it was a family arrangement, honoured and binding, and the child was fed and cared for without payment. It kept the family together. People would give up a lot to look after each other's children. The idea of taking a child away from its family and putting the child in a foster home was generally seen as almost criminal. We were astonished when we first discovered that in England a young mother can be advised to put her child in a foster home because she couldn't get help in bringing it up herself, couldn't even get lodgings because landlords stipulate 'no children'. The family system in Jamaica meant that if you had ten children in your house you had room for another whether or not you were the child's parent. The child stayed till he or she grew up, he accepted his new home, he visited his own parents and spent time with them, and he called the 'mother' in his home 'aunty' or 'grandmother'.

The grandparents are usually at home or very nearby anyway. It was accepted that sons and daughters would look after their own ageing parents. Often in families who are a little better off the children marry and get their own house and the grandparents live in the original family house. Then the new branch of the family would send one of their children to live

75

with the grandparents to keep them company. The nearest daughter would send their meals over and the child run errands, fetch the milk and tobacco for the old people. When we came to England we found it almost impossible to believe that the English put their old people in homes and institutions. It seemed hard and ungrateful. The English did not seem to care about their old people. And if they didn't care for their own old people or their own children, how could they care about immigrants?

But though the Jamaican family is strong and embraces all its members, it is not restrictive. Jamaicans seem to feel a great deal of individual independence. They tend to be assertive too, refuse to be trampled on, and will not be treated as inferior. They rebelled against their masters even when they were in chains and have always opposed any boss who tries to push them down. When we came to England it was with the feeling that it was our right to come. It had then become part of our culture - we had been conditioned to understand and accept it. If rejected we were not then aware of any other culture we could call our own as could say people from India and Pakistan.

It struck at the very roots of our upbringing that some British spoke of their resentment at having their country occupied by strangers. We did not consider ourselves strangers, we had grown up to believe that we were British - children of a mother country we could visit any time, to live, to educate ourselves and to work. We came to England with confidence, that we would not be in a foreign land. We would have come home. It was a shock to be treated as an inferior, inducing strong feelings of despair and being let down. It was like being a favourite son whose mother suddenly rejects him.

In our despair we looked to Africa, which we considered to be a sort of fatherland. When the motherland rejected us we looked to the fatherland to stand up for us. This too proved to be a chimera, we found that many Africans saw us as black colonials. They called us black men with white hearts. They accepted only themselves as true black men, Africans with real identities, cultures and languages, of which they were proud. I, as a Jamaican, admired and envied them, but there were Jamaicans who, in their jealousy of the Africans, despised and rejected them. In those days the African identity appeared lost to us, whilst the European identity was denied to us. Often we tried to be more superior, but underneath we longed to be accepted and loved.

Despite such a whirl of emotions we Jamaicans remained defiant. We asked questions and fought for what we believed in. We were frightened to accept that we were black and different. Even as slaves we had felt ourselves to be human beings and had struggled for the right to be accepted as such. When we came to England we had to fight again, even though our whole self image and identity had been shattered. Often we turned away from thoughts of integration and assimilation, and sought refuge with our own people. On the one hand we longed to go back to our own country, on the other hand we wanted to be respected and belong in this new country. We wanted to write home and tell them proudly that England was a great country and we had bettered ourselves here. We wanted to get back confidence in our own identity for then we knew that, as Jamaicans, we would be loyal and responsible members of the community.

We knew we were creative and resourceful, yet we were treated as inferiors.. When we tried for a room we were told 'no coloureds'; when we went for a job there were suddenly no vacancies; when we opened a newspaper we found it was full of 'the colour problem'. People would say to us: 'Why did you come? Why don't you go home?' Everywhere we turned the door was closed. We were not wanted, so we despaired, we opposed, we struggled. Sometimes we got into trouble. We clung to each other, lived with our own people in a little colony. When we had work we knew our position was precarious, if we came late we would be sacked; if we were early and worked hard we would be turned on by white workers: 'Who do you think you are, trying to steal our jobs?' Either way we were up against it. If we did the right thing we were feared, if we did the wrong thing we were rejected. We could not win. We were driven away, into ourselves, into the ghetto.

There were some Jamaicans who had lived in England for many many years who told me they had never been in an

English home. Many were and are surprised to find I have English friends and am invited to their homes and invite them back to mine. I remember at one party of mine there must have been about fifty people, and only about ten of them were black. One of my Jamaican friends surveyed the scene and turned to me in pleasure and surprise and said: 'Man, you've mixed!' I thought he just about summed it up. He had never seen so many white people at a party before, certainly never in a Jamaican's flat, and yet he had been here for ten years. He had a great time. He found English people talking to him, liking him, dancing with him, drinking with him. He came to see me many times after the party and always talked about it.

'I wish I had so many friends in this country. Weren't they great people! Don't get me wrong. It's not that I don't want to be with Jamaicans. But it's so good to know the other side and to mix like that'. I asked him: 'Why don't you make English friends yourself?' He answered: 'I work with them, ride on the bus with them, then they say "So long! See You tomorrow" and that's that'.

'So why don't you invite them home?'

'I couldn't. They might not come. If I go to a dance I daren't ask an English girl to dance with me. The English boys would look at me and I'd be afraid. So I dance with a black girl.

It was interesting to me that this boy could be so surprised to meet English people in a Jamaican's home. He brought along one of his friends to meet me and we all became friends. Whenever I gave a party I would invite them. Once one of the English girls invited him to one of her parties and before long he was getting invitations to other English parties and he began inviting people back.

The people who came to my parties are the ones who accepted black people in their midst. Sometimes even my English friends were disappointed, they expected to find more Jamaicans but I usually tried to invite a good mixture. I'm certain this is the best way to get better understanding between races. Separation only brings conflict. Each of us must ask: 'Isn't it about time I visited the house next door where my Indian or African neighbour lives?' We are not going to solve any problems by staying in our own houses and with our own kind. And we are not going to do it by laws and committees and preaching. It starts in your own life, in your own house, with the people that you know.

Fourteen

How Would You Like Your Daughter...

Not long after returning from my first sad visit home to Jamaica, I went to see an old RAF friend up in Liverpool. He had asked me to go up and meet his new English wife. We all went to visit the wife's mother while I was there. It was the first time my friend had met his mother-in-law, she had refused to come to the wedding. He told me she had invited him to meet her about a month ago but he hadn't the nerve. I'm sure he asked me to visit them just then so that I could support him.

The mother was a cold serious woman who seemed to me to have had a hurtful life herself. Her first words to her daughter were: 'I wondered whether you were coming or not'. The girl explained we had had to wait for a bus. 'More excuses', said the mother. She didn't greet my friend and took no notice of me whatsoever. When we got inside the house she said: 'Which one of you is the husband?' The girl introduced my friend. 'Are you both from the same country?' My friend was still too nervous to speak so I told her we both came from Jamaica. 'It's funny how you look so different'.

'In what way?' I said.

'You're much darker than him', she said.

'You get dark and not so dark where we come from'.

'Very funny'.

'But mum he's got white blood in him', the girl said, 'He told me his grandparents had some mixture and he is a throwback'.

'So what are you?', the mother turned angrily to my friend, 'Are you half-caste or a quarter?'

He attempted to speak but she went on, 'And what happens when you get her pregnant? What colour will your children be?'

Again the girl replied for him. 'Our children will be nearly white Mum, because if he's only a quarter and my baby's half that means he'll be nearly white'.

I sat on and listened astounded to these two, mother and daughter, discussing in this curious way how much black and white the baby would have. It was so cold. They spoke with no feeling or interest about the child who would be born into the family. I didn't know what to say and I didn't want to interfere but I could sense how my friend was feeling. The mother changed the subject and asked about his job. He managed to tell her he was a mechanic.

'And when do you go back to Jamaica?'

He said he didn't know yet.

'Are you going with him?, she turned back to the girl.

'I don't know. We haven't discussed it'.

'Don't you talk about these things?'

'Give us a chance, Mum. We've only been married a few months'.

'Do you think you'll like living in his country away from us?'

'I won't know till I get there, will I?'

It was cold, right through. I wanted to leave. It wasn't my problem. But my friend implored me to stay. It was late when we returned to their house and the girl was in tears. She told us her mother was like that with everybody first time. 'But I think she'll like you', she said to her husband. Then she went to bed and we sat down again and talked.

'Man, this is a funny country', he said. People up round here say they like coloured folks but they don't really. You marry one and suddenly they don't like you any more. I married her because I love her. I've got a good job and I've got this house and I can provide for her. My folks all want to meet her. They're delighted. This is the first time I've seen her mother and you saw what happened. This is a strange country. They don't seem to think about their children's happiness. Can't they forget their own silly pride for the sake of their own children?'

There wasn't much I could say. 'These are the things you will find, but the most important thing is that you love her. You should be able to fight for her and stand up for her. She'll need you'.

I left next day and returned to London and thought of the sad scene I had witnessed. In one evening, in one hour, in just a word or two, happiness could be destroyed. This girl and her boy had tried so hard. All they needed was for someone close to them to say: 'I wish you well'. But they were denied even that.

Perhaps it was then much harder for the girl. Women depended so much on the personal relationships in their family circle, a man had other possibilities, his job and his public life where he could seek prestige.

I got to know a girl, whom I will call G, very well. We were friends for over five years. Her parents lived far away from London but they got to hear that their daughter was 'going round with a coloured man'. At first her brother came to see us, through curiosity as much as anything, I think. Afterwards, G told me he had reported back to his mother and they both disapproved. However, in time her two sisters came down and seemed to like me and to accept the situation. Soon G's mother herself wrote to me and gradually, through letters, we broke the barrier. During all that time I never met her but I knew enough to feel happy about her views. But if our relationship was to develop I knew there would be other barriers. I was not a Catholic, G was, and she was devoted to her church, attended Mass regularly and got on well with her priest. One day, to my astonishment, I found her in tears when she came to see me. The priest had told her he had heard she was going with a coloured man. He rebuked her and told her she was not being true to her faith, she should marry a Catholic, she should be with people like herself, she wouldn't be happy marrying a coloured man because they had a different way of life. We hadn't seriously contemplated marriage at that stage and I was surprised that he had assumed we would be married. But what really amazed me was that here was a priest, a man of God, a Christian, supposed to be spreading the word that all men are brothers, who was actually saying: 'Don't have him. He's black. Come to church and confess but don't have a black man'.

I thought we had reached beyond this in our life. There were many difficulties for us, mainly due to the ignorance of other people. But when it came to religion I thought that here at least we would find some understanding, that the priest would understand things the man in the street could not. I knew the Catholic Church did not approve of mixed religious marriages, I did not know it also disapproved of mixed racial marriages. Was it unchristian for a black man to marry a white girl?

G wept. She said: 'I believe in my church and I thought its teaching was that we should be friendly with everyone'. She was so upset and confused she could not remember exactly what the priest had said. Did he really mean she should not be with me because I was black or because I was not a Catholic? I told her to go back and ask him. But she never had the opportunity. Whenever she went to see him she tried to bring it out but he silenced her and said: 'Remember my child, I'm only thinking of your future happiness'. G said she would leave the church but I knew her religion was important to her still. I was thinking of her future too, and my own. I knew it would always come between us. Gradually the relationship ended.

Since then I have known many couples happy at the start whose lives together were broken by racial and family pressures.

In Jamaica, marriage between Negroes, Indians, Chinese, Europeans was normal. Members of the same family might be of different colours and have different racial characteristics, but there was no special belief that one colour was better than another. People are different, as are flowers, trees and animals. We worried less about classification than people in other countries. We had had a long history of mixed marriage and had shown that it worked and was a natural part of the life of a community.

It only becomes a problem when the community believes it to be so. It was another of the shocks that hit us when we came to England.

An English friend of mine married a Jamaican girl who had come here to be a nurse. He married her because he loved her. But two days before the wedding he told me he had decided they would eventually go and live in Jamaica because he was not sure how long he would be able to keep his job once it became known he had married a coloured girl. But his feeling for her was greater than his worry about his job and the marriage was very happy at the beginning.

She remained in her nursing training and he went on with his job as a chemist. But he never let anyone from work meet his wife. When they left the house for work in the morning, she went in one direction and he in the other, and they came home by separate routes and at different times. They only met inside the house.

He was the only son of parents with two daughters and was separated from his family. None of them had come to the wedding. Now he wanted to know if they would accept his wife. He tried to find out on a visit home by himself. His sisters were hostile, his mother indifferent and his father said nothing. He felt a stranger to the family, yet to me he had always seemed to be a fellow who needed his parents near. He was brought up to be dependent on them and his marriage did not help to break the dependence. In fact, it showed up the fact that he needed them more. Things began to get difficult between him and his wife. She came to see me in tears one day and asked me to talk to him. She wanted to meet his friends. She had kept up with all her coloured friends but she didn't know a single white, English girl. Her marriage had not led to friendship with her husband's family or his friends. He was beginning to find fault with her. She worked too long at the hospital, she didn't care about him and their home, her cooking was bad. She got so down that eventually the hospital asked her to leave. She wasn't getting to work on time and could not give enough attention to her studies or to the patients. She gave up a job she loved and decided to stay at home. Perhaps this would show him that she loved him. But it wasn't enough. Several times she asked me to talk to him. But it is difficult to reach a man who is cut off. He felt he was floating in air, nowhere, he had no links and no roots. He accused her of causing the break with his family. It was because of her he could not see his parents, and his sisters would not visit him. He went down and down and eventually the marriage broke up. She returned to Jamaica, sad and confused. She never really knew why it happened.

The pressures brought to bear on individuals by their families and by society can be harsh and uncompromising. But sometimes the individual hits back and uses the same pressures to attack his family and society. A young woman I knew whose parents were quite wealthy persistently failed her exams and did badly at school, in spite against her father who set great store by intellectual success. She never felt as good as her elder sister, so she found ways of attacking her family. At first she tried to belittle them by getting into trouble with the neighbours. Then she left home and took to cafe life, taking drugs and sleeping around. She met a West African student and eventually married him. Her parents knew nothing about it. The marriage began to fail after the first few weeks. He loved her right enough but he told me: 'I'm not sure if she loves me. I don't really know why she wanted to marry'.

He mixed mainly with his own people and she began to involve herself with the African immigrant community. Soon she began asking herself whether the marriage would hold. She told me one day: 'I think I married him just to spite my parents'. To make herself more acceptable to her new friends she took to wearing West African clothes. He didn't like this. 'I married an English girl', he told me, 'Why does she go around pretending to be African? I want her to be English'.

She certainly looked odd in African clothes. And the African girls turned their backs on her. This upset her most. No-one accepted her. She was trying to attack her parents, her own way of life, and this battle was so important to her that the marriage stood no chance. The quarrelling got bitter. She would say she wore his people's clothes so that she could be near him. But she was mocking him and his people as her real purpose was to attack her own people. The marriage ended quickly. It had never really begun.

Immigrants could often find themselves with people like this, people kicking against their own kind, girls seeking out coloured boy friends only to defy their parents and to spite boys of their own colour. When the reality of marriage tested the relationship they found they were not in love at all. The social weapon of colour prejudice was turned against the society which bred it. The marriage would break down and people took this as the proof they needed that mixed marriages did not work. They never looked for the real reason which lay inside themselves. This would have meant a heart searching which would uncover their own prejudice.

Fifteen

Mr Ferron Is a Black Man Too

In my work as a social worker, as well as in my private life, it is not unusual for people to talk to me about black people quite bluntly and without any embarrassment to them or pain for me. Often I find people so full of colour prejudice and so in need to talk it out that paradoxically they do not seem to see that I am black too. To them I am just another friend of the family. I remember my contact with one family whose young daughter got into all kinds of trouble with men. Her mother was particularly upset and bitter one day when I went round to see them.

'My daughter is pregnant by a coloured man! A coloured man, Mr Ferron!'

I was not all that surprised. She went on: 'There's plenty of fellows in the street, white and black, and I know the white ones aren't much cop in this area but that would have been better than with a black man'. Her face grimaced in disgust as she said it. I listened to her outpouring and when she paused for a moment I told her I shared her disappointment that the girl was pregnant but now it had happened she would need her mother's help.

She must see that she wouldn't have to face it alone.

'But what about the people in the street?' the mother said, 'How do you think they will react when they know? She's not married. That's bad enough but having a black baby is worse'.

'The neighbours will talk anyway', I said, 'That's something we all have to live with. But the important thing now is that she mustn't feel rejected'.

'Well she can't stay here! There's no room for a baby. And when her father hears of it he'll throw her out'.

I murmured something about hoping they would see their responsibilities a bit more constructively instead of just responding to their own immediate disgust, and I offered to talk with her father as I knew him well. A few days later they invited me over again. All three of them were there and the father had already been told.

'I don't want a little black bastard in my house! You can take it and go and live with him whoever he is'.

The girl was embarrassed. 'But Dad, Mr Ferron is a black man too. How do you think he feels when you say things like that?'

'Mr Ferron is Mr Ferron as far as I'm concerned'.

And it was true. I was Mr Ferron, who worked with the family; they had a problem and had asked me to share it with them. It just so happened that the problem was their daughter having a black baby. I went into some detail with her father about how important it was for him to concern himself with the girl's future and not to reject her but to give her a chance to prove herself. They talked about abortion but they decided there would not be enough grounds. Tempers cooled a little as we talked and the discussion turned into a sober exercise between the parents and myself. I said I would talk to the young man if they thought it would help and the girl said she would arrange it for the following Monday.

I met him and he turned out to be the kind of fellow I hoped would never leave the West Indies, arrogant, indifferent and casual, the kind who creates trouble and gives all black immigrants a bad name.

'Why should I talk to you? What are you anyway? Some kind of protector of the young?'

I said I was a friend of the family and told him to sit down and listen. If he wanted to prove he was a man, now was the time. What was he going to do about it?

He said nothing, then: 'How do you know the kid's mine?'

I said I didn't know, only he and the girl knew that, but we had been told the child was his and I wanted to know what he was going to do to help. Could he help pay for its upkeep, for instance. He agreed he would. He even put it in writing.

When I saw the family again they were surprised and relieved he had agreed to pay something. It would help because they were a poor family, but they also needed help to accept the fact that their daughter was pregnant and unmarried and that they would have a black grandchild. Gradually, the mother managed to hold down her fear of the neighbours and the pregnancy took its course and the girl gave birth to a fine healthy boy. The parents visited her every day in hospital and took her and the baby back home when the time came. Also her father began to take to the baby. 'My grandson', he would say, 'You may be a little black bastard but you're my first grandson'.

His elder daughter was married but had no children. As he began to move towards the new baby she became jealous and wanted to share in. The young mother resented her interference. We were facing a new problem. I could only help by trying to get them all to discuss it instead of quarrelling and then avoiding each other. The girl had to see her sister's gesture as helpful and accepting, that she was not rejecting her but wanted to share with her. Soon the girl got herself a job and the grandmother gave up her own job to look after the baby. Help came for the girl, late but in time.

I looked up another family I had not seen for some time. I soon discovered a tension in the house. No-one would talk straight with the others. Somehow my presence seemed to loosen their tongues. We had many discussions over several days and it was during one of these that I discovered that some of the tension had to do with the daughter's friendship with a black boy. The mother had just said: 'My sister is coming down from the North next week so I hope you won't bring your boyfriend round on Monday. You know how she feels about coloured people'. It seemed to be a way of letting me know the situation without actually telling me directly. So I casually asked: 'Does your daughter know some coloured boys then?'

'Didn't you know?', the father broke in, 'She's all over them.

He came here the other night. Got the shock of my life when I walked in here and saw him. Looked like one of those blacks who go round selling ties. And would you believe it, he was sitting in my chair! No-one asked me. Doesn't matter what I think round here. There he was, sitting in my chair'.

'There was nowhere else for him to sit, Dad. And he'd only just come a minute before you did. I was going to introduce you but you never gave me a chance. You just stood there shouting your head off'.

'Them kind I don't mix with, and I won't have them in the house. I don't care what you do outside, but don't bring them here'.

The mother said: 'I'd rather she brought them here than end up in Brixton and them places'.

'If she chooses to go with that lot it's up to her to take what comes', the father said.

'Your wife has a point though,' I said, 'If she brings her boyfriends home you don't have to worry about where she is or who she's with.

'Can't stand some of these West Indians. They live in the Labour Exchange. Never seen any of them do a days work. Hanging around the streets all hours. And I won't have them coming in here. You don't know where they've come from. I haven't got much that's valuable here but what I've got I don't want pinched'.

'He's not a thief!' The girl jumped up and stood over her father. But again it was the mother who dropped the bomb.

'Well after all', she began, reasonably, 'If she's going to marry him I think we ought to start being a bit more friendly. He's not bad really and unless we take to him there's no knowing what they might do. Young people these days don't think about their parents. They end up doing all sorts of things'.

The father exploded: 'Marry him!'

'Hasn't she told you then?'

'No, she bloody well hasn't!'

The girl was defiant. 'What's wrong with that?' The poor man was speechless. So I came in.

'Children often seem to like people their parents don't. But in this case you don't even know the chap. You've never talked to him. Don't you think you ought to wait till you have before you pass judgement?'

'What? Meet him? Would you let your daughter marry a black man?' He was so angry, so at the mercy of his feelings that he'd forgotten I was black. He'd forgotten who I was. These things were suddenly irrelevant. The girl started to giggle. He turned on her.

'What the hell are you laughing at then?'

'If you could just see your face, Dad, you'd laugh too. You say some daft things sometimes, don't you?'

'What the hell do you mean?' He really didn't know.

'You asking Mr Ferron if he would let his daughter marry a black man'. And then he saw. And he said quickly: 'He knows what I mean. And he'd feel the same if he was in my position'.

'Well, he isn't, is he?' the mother said, 'And you're making it very awkward for him. How would you feel if you was in his position?'

He turned to me. 'I don't mean educated ones like you. It's them with the flashy ties and trousers I can't stand. And I won't have her mixing with them'.

At that point the son came in. The mother told him his tea was in the kitchen but he came in and sat down.

'What's up with you lot then? You all look a bit upset'.

'It's about Nick', the girl said.

'Oh? What's wrong with Nick?'

'What's wrong with him? Are you bloody blind?' the father burst out again.

'I'm not blind. But I don't see anything wrong with him. I know him and I know his sister. They came with us last time we went on a ramble. And she's coming here to tea next week. She's nice, Dad'.

'Blimey! Don't tell me you've taken up with this lot too!'

'What's wrong with them?' the boy asked again.

And out it all exploded again. Finally the boy challenged his father. 'Look Dad. You're saying who we should mix with and who we shouldn't. But look at your friends. Look at the types you mix with. You meet them in the pub but you think you're better than they are, and you never bring them to the house. I can't understand you at all. And when we choose our friends you don't like them. Nick's sister is ten times better than the lot you mix with. You wait till you see her, Dad. She's smashing!'

'That's it for me. You can all do what you like. Don't ask me. This is no place for me'. And he got up to walk out. But the mother stopped him.

'No, we've got to thrash it out here, now, while Mr Ferron's here. Because if we don't now, we never will and it will happen again and all you'll do is shout'.

So everyone settled down again. I began to feel sorry for the man. His two children were forcing him to look at himself. His wife would not support him, not because she had no prejudice against the coloured boyfriend or because she wanted to go against her husband but because her girl was unhappy. So the poor man was surrounded; his wife was not his ally, his daughter loved a coloured man, his son thought the man's sister was 'smashing', and I was there, neutral, wanting to help them all, but black. He couldn't win.

I turned the talk back to his own friends. Why did he not bring them home?

'Who can I bring here?', he said shaking his head, 'There's old Bill down there. He walked out on his old woman because she took up with another bloke. I can't bring him because all he talks about is his old woman. Then there's Charlie. Married a woman from up North, he did. And where's she now? Gone off. And I don't blame her. He drinks too much'.

'So you know what it's like not being able to bring your friends home. You can't see what Bill sees in his wife and you're not surprised Charlie's wife left him. What would you say if Charlie was black? Would you say it was a good thing she left him?'

'Yes, if he drinks the way he does'.

'What if she was white and he was coloured?'

'Well, a woman ought to have her head tested marrying a bloke like him in the first place'. He avoided the real question, but at least we were talking.

'Either way the prejudice is there', I said, 'You're prejudiced against them and against your daughter's friends because you don't think they're good enough'.

'Yes, but they're white and this is colour'.

'What's different? You've never seen this boy behaving badly. If he wears a loud tie, that's all you have to go on'.

'Well how would you like to come home of an evening and find one of those lazy black bastards sitting in your chair?'

He'd forgotten me again, but it didn't matter.

'You've got a duty to your daughter'. I played it heavy now. 'You've got to accept that she's got her own life and it may not go the way you think it should. If she chooses someone you don't like only because he's black, don't you think you're imposing on her life? You aren't helping her. And you won't get it your way because you'll just make her bitter. You'll push her away telling her you don't want her'.

'I love my daughter!' he protested.

'Is this the way to show it? You asked me what I would do if I was in your position. I would call the boy and talk with him. I would sit on my prejudice. And if I couldn't I'd tell him: 'I don't like coloured people myself but if you and my daughter are happy it's enough for me'. You have to be honest and let the couple know that though you don't like the situation you aren't going to destroy it. Because you'll destroy yourself too. You won't get your way, because you'll just drive her from you and closer to him'.

A pause, and the son came in. 'You ought to go to some coloured parties Dad'.

'Not bleeding likely'.

'No, straight up Dad. You'd enjoy it. They have a way about them with music, the way they move to it. It's so different from us. First time I met a coloured boy I didn't know how to talk to him and we went and played badminton. And he was very good. I wanted to learn to play like that and he showed me. I always envied the way they move. They seem to have it in their bones. This chap took me to a coloured club and it wasn't a bit like what they say. And I met his mum and dad, and they're nice folks'.

The boy brought in something new. And it had a curious effect. The father calmed down and then began to feel guilty about me.

'I hope you don't think I'm prejudiced. You've helped us. But the way this country is going, you can't blame me for being careful'.

'I don't blame you', I said.

As it turned out, the girl went on seeing her boyfriend. He visited the house several times and the father let her have a party and invite her black friends. At one time the two youngsters talked about getting engaged but it never came to anything. The son went on seeing the sister but that never got serious either. The important thing was that the family held together and began to rearrange their life.

The colour prejudice of the ordinary, often economically disadvantaged, families I usually worked with was of the vague, unthinking sort which could be dispelled as personal contact became more strongly established. But sometimes I met, and still meet, people in the so called 'educated' classes whose prejudice is more firmly entrenched and articulated. It is embarrassing enough for them to accept the help they know they need because it means facing their own feelings of failure, but when the advice or help is offered by a professional black man there is no escape for them.

I remember an ex-army officer whose house I had to visit in connection with some advice and information about his young child who had learning difficulties. The house was in a well-to-do part of London. I went up and rang the bell. He came out, surly and brusque.

'What do you want?'

I introduced myself and told him why I had called.

'Why did they send you? Couldn't they find a white fellow to send?'

I said this area happened to be the one I worked in as a social worker.

'I don't like you people so it's a waste of time talking, isn't it?'

'I don't think so. I may be able to help you if you can spare me a minute. The fact that you don't like me doesn't prevent me from talking to you or helping you if I can.

He asked me where I was from and I told him.

'Served with some of you fellows in the Army. Had you in the Far East, and some Indians. All you fellows are damned good fighters once you've been trained. The bastards do their job well but once they go back home they go right back to their tribal ways. They're basically very primitive. Doesn't matter what education they've had. They still go back to the old way of life'.

'Why don't you like them?'

'Got no reason to. Talked to them because I had to'.

Then he challenged me directly: 'What do you feel when I say I don't like you blacks?'

'It doesn't bother me. I have no reason to like you either. In fact, your attitude makes me feel I don't like you at all'.

He reacted strongly: 'How dare you!' I wondered myself why I'd said it. In my mind I thought I shouldn't have. But he didn't slam the door.

'Do you always go around telling people you don't like them?'

'No. But you asked me. You've already told me you didn't like me so I had to be as honest with you too'.

It was raining at the time, so his wife came to the door and said: 'Why do you stand there in the rain, why don't you come inside'.

I was surprised at this, but we went in and sat down. He started telling me all about his army career. He seemed to be quite bitter about most things. Eventually we were able to discuss the difficult situation about his child and then he offered me some tea.

'You're one of the educated ones'. But he was sceptical about how far coloured people could use their education. He went on again about how they always go back to their 'tribal ways', 'back to the jungle', but I had a feeling that he was just reciting what he had heard from other people. It wasn't from his own experience. We finished the tea and I was ready to go. He said at the door: 'Enjoyed our chat. If you happen to be passing this way again don't forget to call on me'.

He surprised me again. But when I thought about it, it seemed he was a man who had to be challenged on his own terms with confidence. He wanted to find out for himself that I could do the job because my colour told him I couldn't. He had to test it for himself. I wondered if I had done the correct thing telling him I didn't like him. He needed advice and my response to him was hardly professional. It was the first time in a professional situation that I had ever told someone I didn't like them. I decided I would never say it again, but it had seemed to serve its purpose on that occasion. The man had repeated many times what he thought about coloured people. He demanded a response and he got it.

There are some people who test you out and you can deal with it and smile. But when an intelligent experienced person tries to belittle you and talks about the colonies and subjection, that inferiority is something inherited by coloured races and will never be removed, you have to meet him square on. You have to prove your own confidence because this is what he wants to see before he starts to trust you and, perhaps, begins to understand you.

Certainly my blackness brings out colour prejudice, but when it does, and only then, I have the chance to tackle it, not as my problem but as the problem of those who harbour it. But my professional colleagues always believe it must be a problem for me. This subtle form of prejudice used to irritate me. Now I am merely amused as I wait for the doubts to come out: 'Do people accept you? Do you become conscious of your colour when you visit homes. Does it affect the way you work?' Always this constant reminder from professional people I meet for the first time. This is the first thing they ask. Not about my ability, not about my experience, but my colour, always my colour. They are so sure it prevents me from doing my job. It doesn't. It is part of my job and that's how I tackle it. The people I work with are usually so engrossed in their own troubles, and so in need, that for them the only relevant question is not my colour but can I help them.

Sixteen

All They Are Saying

I look back over my many years in this country and see how it has changed. It is not so much that the colour problem is worse, it is a different problem now. There was not the mass awareness of the presence of black people when I first came as there is now. Much more is written, said, and seen which inflames the situation even though the intention may be the opposite. Forty years and more ago it was individual prejudice. You could walk along the street and no one would worry you. They might look, even stare. The constant reminder that you were black and different was always there but you didn't feel it so much *all* the time. But I would say it became far worse for black people in the sixties because there was more awareness and, therefore, more immediate fear. We were confronted with it all day and every day, in the shops, at the factory, in the laundry, in the schools, in the street, on the trains and buses. There was this constant discussion. You read about it, you were asked about it. Perhaps there was no more real discrimination then than before but the problem was out in the open. This was the difference. And it was not a bad thing in itself that eyes should be opened to the fact there were black communities in the country. But it is the way the eyes were opened that was wrong. Earlier I wrote about the way the newspapers influenced attitudes to black troops during the war. The papers were still full of stories, not now to help white people to accept us but to inflame the situation. Stories about the numbers of immigrants here, and of those arriving, were distorted. Reporters interviewed people in the street: 'What do you feel about having coloured people living beside you, working alongside you?' The way the questions were asked put fear into the minds of people. So the moment a coloured family took a house in the street or a black person turned up for work, people began to ask themselves: 'What do I feel about this?' It disturbed especially the ones who could not think for themselves and who merely recited what the papers and politicians said. They reacted accordingly, they protested.

I remember on a visit to Leicester talking to a man who told me that a black family had lived in his street for over ten years. As far as he was concerned they were just another set of neighbours. But quite suddenly, since the publicity, he found himself noticing them more and other people in the street talking about them. His neighbour had recently said to him: 'Did you know we had coloureds in the street?' He reminded her that the family had been there for ten years and that she herself had been there for eight, but it was only now that she had *really* seen them.

By the late fifties, when the problem was beginning to develop into a crisis I felt that a lot of the work I and thousands of other immigrants were doing was being overlooked. I was terribly afraid of the influence of the newspapers, the fears they created in the mind. I set out to talk to my friends and to people I met, maybe reassure them about their doubts and respond to their queries. I wished there had been more planning for the arrival of immigrants. They should never have been allowed to come and settle without a job. I never did agree with this. They stepped down from the boat or off the plane straight into the hands of the dishonest who exploited them. I believed it would be a long time before coloured immigrants were accepted. There was still so much ignorance. People ought to have been given much more information.

It seemed the only time black people appeared on television was when there was some trouble. Then certain political extremists always seemed to get the limelight. Reporters went out of their way to seek out black people who are intensely anti-white. This annoyed and often frightened white people even more and reinforced prejudice and ignorance. Immigrants were so sick of watching old films on television that depicted the white interpretation of a backward Africa with people wearing loin cloths and tribal marks on their faces. There was no attempt to examine traditions within the appropriate cultural context and very little attempt to show the modern new states, except when they were in some political crisis.

In a country with so many thousands of people from the West Indies there should be much more factual information about their way of life and the islands they come from, that they do not live in the trees, that they go shod not barefoot, that they go clothed not naked or in rags. I brought a film back from Jamaica and showed it to some friends. The first comment was: 'I never realised you had beautiful highways like that'. This quite intelligent Englishman did not know we had such roads in Jamaica. His one brief statement told me so much.

People want to know who they are opening their door to. The stranger does not get a fair introduction to the country because the people who have been asked to take him in know so little about him. If they knew more perhaps they would be less suspicious. I believe that with guidance, sane thinking and intelligent government, difficulties can be overcome. But I have inside me some doubt about whether the majority of black people believe this. In the 1960s we were being poisoned by the negative propaganda, being influenced to think that violence might be the means by which to effect change. We listened to the extremists, white and black, because we were already frustrated and half believed what they had to say. I feared the power movements in the black community. I believed in a collective union of immigrants discussing and preparing ways of making themselves accepted, to pass through the gate without breaking the lock. I felt it was no use ganging up against a hostile environment, or living entirely within our culture so avoiding the native population.

Fear of violence was common among immigrant parents. Many feared their youngsters would become involved in violence, that the 'colour' problem was so acute that violence would be the only way. This was a gloomy prospect. Violence only occurs if it is allowed to happen. It is people who cause violence, people in responsible positions who make irresponsible speeches, people in positions of leadership who cannot truly lead. I did not believe that the politician, who spoke against black immigrants and invited the white hosts to turn against them, spoke for all England, not even for most of it. Conversely many immigrants from the Caribbean had positive views about some areas of their life in this new country. I have often heard West Indians say they would rather work under a white foreman because a black foreman would be too strict, and that they believed a black policeman would be harder on them. Yet I was doubtful about how many of the newer immigrants would remain here, especially the young ones. West Indians have always been thinking of going back.

In the sixties, I remember talking to a group of Jamaican schoolgirls due to leave school. One said: 'I've been accepted for a job but I'm afraid to go. When I went for interview the other girls giggled at me'.

'Why did they do that?'

'It's because I'm coloured'.

'How do you know? And why are you so conscious of your colour?'

'Everywhere you go people are on about it all the time'.

'Your employer seems to accept you though?'

'Oh yes. He gave me the job, didn't he? But I noticed that when a white girl came out of her interview before me he walked to the door with her and opened it for her. But when my interview was over he just said he would be writing to me'.

'Maybe he already knew the other girl'.

'Maybe. But I'm still afraid. I wish I didn't have to go there. I wish I could find a job with more coloured girls. I don't want to be the only one'.

I asked the others what they thought. They all felt the same. One said: 'I went for a job and they all started talking differently from what I'm used to and I couldn't understand them. And when I asked them to explain they just looked at me as if I was stupid'.

'But why couldn't you understand them? Did they speak too quickly?'

'No, it wasn't that. I think they deliberately talked that way so I wouldn't understand'.

'Did you get the job though?' She said she was still waiting for a reply. 'But I don't think they want us there really. I don't think I shall get it and I'm not sure if I want it anyway'. I tried to tell her that if she went there expecting rejection she might well get rejected. But she said: 'I want to go home really'. She told me she had left there when she was two years old.

'And you've been here for fourteen years. You don't know Jamaica'.

'But I still want to go back'.

I asked the others what they thought. One said: 'I'm not afraid to stay here. I'm just worried about my mother, she's too strict. The English mothers aren't like that. My English friend's mother lets her go out in the evening but my mother won't let me. She says she doesn't like the company I keep. But she doesn't know my company and I just wish she wouldn't be so strict'.

But another girl had other ideas: 'I wouldn't like my mother to be easy like the English mothers. I like her to be strict because it helps me'. It was interesting. One girl had already accepted a society where the mothers were more permissive with their daughters and the other wanted to keep the traditional stricter customs because this showed that her mother cared what happened to her. Another girl said she didn't like English girls or their mothers. 'They won't come to my house to play records because their mothers won't let them. It's because I'm coloured and they're white'.

'How do you know that?'

'They told me so themselves'.

These youngsters were full of conflict. They lived in a 'black' home environment with black friends. The house, the furniture, the food, the people, the whole framework of their lives were all West Indian. When they came home from school they came home to Jamaica or wherever; when they went to school in the morning they went to England. We expected them to live this split life without help. And who could help them?

I spoke to their teachers. One male teacher told me: 'I have a class of West Indian girls. They are all inadequate. They won't have much chance in this country. It's bad enough to be coloured but to be inadequate as well will be too much'.

I asked him what he meant by 'inadequate'.

'I think it's the way they must have been treated in other schools when they were younger. They were all born here and it shocks me to see how colour conscious they are. Their recorded educational standard is below other girls yet they are bright. They must have had some bad times with their teachers, or maybe outside school or maybe they've been influenced by what they've seen on television or something. *But as a result they've lost heart* and they've never got on'.

Another teacher agreed with him. 'I love my girls. They're very bright and so beautiful. Very interesting children to teach. But it worries me to find how much colour feeling they all have'.

It was worrying but not surprising. The youngsters born in this country were born into colour prejudice. It was seen as part of life.

A youth leader I spoke to was very proud of his club but reluctant to be drawn into an explanation of why he had no coloured members. 'One comes occasionally but he's not a member. He comes with a group and they play tennis. He's very good at it'.

'Why have you no coloured members?'

'Don't ask me. It's nothing to do with me. I've got nothing against them personally, I have to go by what the majority of the boys say. If they don't want coloured members there's nothing I can do about it'.

'But don't you ever try to guide the boys? You're a youth leader, you're not running a therapeutic group. I would have thought you would be concerned to help all youth'.

'It's all very well for you to talk. You don't live round here. I've got nothing against them. I'm not proud I haven't got any coloured members, but I'm not sorry either. I don't understand the boys who want them in. I just don't want to know'.

'What about the coloured boys who've got nowhere to go?'

'It's sad for them, I know. I don't know how they manage. They should form their own clubs'.

'That would be segregation wouldn't it?'

'It needn't be. They could invite their white friends if they wanted to'.

I was sad to hear him. This was an area where a lot of work could be done, but not if the clubs were run by leaders like him. Another youth club leader told me two coloured boys had been to his club once but had never returned. He didn't know why. 'I suppose the other boys weren't very friendly. I run a decent club. I don't mind their colour as long as they behave themselves. I don't know what my boys feel'.

I asked him what sort of future the immigrant children had. 'They're in for a hard time, I'm sure. It's going to get more difficult for them'. I talked to a policeman. The police are more exposed to criticism than other people; if they have prejudice it's much harder for them to hide it. 'You can't rule out your own feelings or your prejudices,' he said, 'But I think it makes me put more effort into making sure that justice is done. I like the coloured boys, they're a good lot really but I wish they wouldn't go around in gangs'.

'They're always in a group and it just makes them look suspicious somehow. I've stopped some of them sometimes and they always look scared, guilty somehow even though they may not be. Some of my colleagues have had some rough experiences but I never have. I've worked in Brixton and there's no more trouble there than anywhere else. I don't know what it's like elsewhere. But some of you fellows get into trouble with the law. It's this careless attitude you have about passing drugs, smoking pot. That's why people suspect you. But it's usually people who don't know any coloured folk themselves. I know a coloured family now. The boy goes to school with my son. When he found out I was a policeman he was scared and his parents told him not to come to our house. But my son went over to their house and the two boys went on being friends. And now his father has been over to see me. He works in a garage, very good mechanic too. I take my car there and he repairs it so I know. They're good folks. Not well off, just trying. I see a lot of coloured folks trying very hard'.

I asked him if the police were worried about the influx of

immigrants. 'If immigrants cause us trouble, it's not because they're coloured, it's just that they're different and don't know our ways. It's easier if they speak English though'.

A probation officer told me he hadn't come across many coloured delinquents but he had a feeling that there were going to be a lot more when the youngsters left school and found they could not get jobs. 'There are plenty of ways of getting round the Race Relations legislation'. And it's then that they may turn to violence.

A twelve year old black boy lad told me: 'I love Jamaica, when I grow up I shall go back there'. I reminded him he had been born here, how did he know what Jamaica was like. 'My dad was born there so that's my home. I don't want to live here'.

Another boy told me: 'The white boys in my class can't play cricket and I don't like football. I'm going to play for the West Indies one day but if I don't get enough practice I won't be good enough. So I'm going home to get some real practice'.

The children who talked to me may have been too young to do more than speak out their fears and feelings. But the way they said things caused anxiety to those of us who were trying to help them grow up. Their world was immediately in front of them and they saw it with a child's clarity. They had already decided that life in England was not for them. My only hope was that if they returned to the West Indies they would not go for the wrong reasons. A white business man who was of Jamaican nationality told me that white people in Jamaica would be horrified if they had knew about the current feelings towards black people in England. 'I just hope the Jamaicans who return will remember that the white Jamaicans do not feel like the white people in England'. Much of what he told me echoed my fears that young people who returned angry with the white English would turn against white Jamaicans.

The black families who remained in England needed assurance that they were not regarded as inferiors who took bread, work, houses, school places and hospital beds from the white population. Conversely, the white population needed to know their position was not threatened. In those days one of the biggest provocations to white people was the sight of a black person in the offices of the then Ministry of Social Security. The attitude was: 'These people have come to take our money'. This prevalent view knew nothing of the agony, the pain in the heart, when the immigrant had to do this. The West Indians' life was hard, they knew that it was only by hard work that they would survive. When they had to go and ask for money they were going backwards; they came here to go forwards. They had taken a backward step because their confidence had been destroyed by the ignorance and rejection of other people. The trials of getting a job were multiplied by reactions to their colour. They were already fearful about not getting jobs without the further harm caused as a result of being rejected simply for being black, thus being denied any opportunity to grow. These conflicts bred feelings of being inferior, unsuccessful, unacceptable, that no-one really cared and that anyone who did, did so because they felt sorry. This was possibly the most hateful thing of all. They didn't want pity. Black people were proud, dignified people struggling against feelings of inferiority imposed on them by a dominant white society.

Generally I found it was the men who wanted to stay and fight for their rights, and it was the women who wanted to return home. The mothers were so fearful for their young. I always felt that black children must be allowed to grow up and find their own way with white children. I thought that may be they could work it out for themselves. Possibly the danger was not so great as some politicians, and journalists would have us believe. When fear is created without real cause, if one is told there will be a disaster one begins to expect it, to wait for it to happen, to believe it will happen and, because one believes it, it does happens - it becomes a self-fulfilling prophesy.

Yet many child care officers and health visitors and other social workers told me how much they respected working with black families. Housing was a bigger difficulty than money because the men worked hard and often the women worked too. But it was usual to find a family with four or five children sharing one room. The homes were clean and the children quiet mannered and well dressed, but the houses were old and crumbling with neglect. The struggle to maintain standards in such an environment often got the women down and many became severely depressed. Often they did not know what help was available and when they did they were too timid to ask for it. In any case their pride, and more especially their husbands' pride, held them back.

It was always the black person who had to control his feelings and his involvement. Certainly this was always my experience. You often felt like smacking someone in the eye, but you talked to him instead. It was no good demonstrating the same ignorance and violence that people showed to you. You had to take their ignorance in hand and turn it into knowledge and sense. When you meet rejection you don't turn back, you try to go forward. If you get despondent and turn back from the first door that is slammed in your face you will never reach the second. The first door is the beginning, not the end.

Seventeen

It Is a Beginning

Was there something wrong with the white people who settled in other lands during the days of imperialism? Did the sons of England need the protection of imperial greatness? Did they really feel so exposed and threatened in distant lands? Is that why they had to keep separate from native peoples? And did their past glory, built perhaps on their own inferiority, serve only to keep that inferiority at bay, enabling them to maintain an outward superiority over black peoples? Is this why there was a whites-only policy in Australia, a segregationist policy in the southern states of North America, the complete suppression of the black man in South Africa? - countries that are English speaking with cultures and customs mainly of English origin. It can be no accident that colour prejudice is stronger in them. I don't know. But it worries me, it worries me greatly as it does most black people and, I hope, some white people too.

The present state of mind is rooted in hundreds of years of conditioning to the belief that black people are inferior to white people. This persistent humiliation over the centuries has built strong attitudes in white and black alike. The black people were the slaves and servants of the white masters and the nurses to his children. Is it possible for the grandchildren of the white masters to regard the grandchildren of their slaves as anything but inferior? But former slaves grew beyond their past and black people came to consider themselves equal to the grandchildren of the white masters. They were even encouraged to believe this by the very same white masters - to forget the past, to advance their own countries, and to look to the future with hope and pride. Then they came to England and found that white people 'at home' still regarded them as they did a hundred years ago and knew nothing of their way of life. The reality came as a shock to both parties. White people feared these black people. They felt cheated. The immigrants did not cause prejudice, they have only brought out the prejudice that was already there.

Despite this I have abundant trust and love for the people of this country and believe that their sense of fair play will turn the rising tide of black and white extremism. Some will reach for the extremes because of their own fears. But in recent times the British have demonstrated their intolerance of tyranny and their demands for justice and fair play for the individual. I cannot believe that these same people, so rich in history, so renowned for law and order, the creators of so many enduring human institutions, will allow the forces of evil to spread in their own land. Race and colour became, and are still, a significant problem in British society. Excuses won't solve the difficulties. Looking back into history won't solve them either. Perhaps not even reason and knowledge will solve them. We have to look into the hearts of people.

Racial prejudice is a reality in England. The immigration laws, the utterances of some politicians and the behaviour of some of those who have the power to give or deny rights to the citizen, confront us with this unmistakable reality. Ill-informed publicity has upset many well-meaning English people and given ammunition to the extremists. It was this that was responsible for me taking the decision to write my own story.

It all began with the romantic notions of a black boy and his glorious dreams of England, his discoveries when he came here; then, as he awakened from his dream into reality, it tells of his disappointments, his hopes, his anger, his love, his rejection, his beliefs, his reconstruction and his integration. I have watched an old England pass by and a new England emerge. I have seen black boys dying, I have seen English boys dying, united as equals in death. Now what I want is for us to be equal when we are alive. I have never been allowed to feel that this is so. I am told I may marry whoever I love, but there is resentment if she is white; I must send my children to school so that they may learn, it is the law of the land, but I am told my children are filling the places in the classroom and pushing out white children; I am told I should live decently in a clean house, but I must not buy a house in a decent, clean neighbourhood; I am told I must work, I want to work, but I am refused work because I am black. These are the contradictions that blacks have to live with. What are the remedies? Re-education, a more even redistribution of black people, more schools, more youth centres, more and truer information and publicity? Perhaps. But there is also more to be done by the person-to-person contact which I have always advocated.

I know the road is hard and there is a long way to go.

The first forty years and more were a beginning for me, forty years of intense continuous involvement, of finding out how to be and what to do, of trying to understand the differences between white and black and how to make the two colours work and live in harmony. It is sad that one had to spend forty years on these things only to say now that it was a beginning. If I had my time over again I would still have joined the RAF and come to this country. I would still have stayed after the war. I might tackle the early rejections differently, but the way I did deal with them taught me how to deal with those I met later. If I now tackled them with the hate and anger as I did then I would be considered a racial extremist. My philosophy is based on my own conflicts, my thoughts and my enquiries. I am beginning to learn how to make this philosophy work. It is *after* you have done everything you can to integrate yourself that the real problems begin, when you try to live up to it, what it does to you in relation to your own people, the fears it brings you. I often go among black friends and find I do not belong. I do not want to lose my own identity. I cannot, and will not, be allowed to forget that I am a foreigner. I must therefore be true to myself as I move forwards.

I have learned to control something very basic to every West Indian, especially to the Jamaican. Self control is so difficult for people from 'new countries'. The new freedom after so many centuries of suppression and restriction releases boundless energy. The English are free, but their freedom comes from centuries of discipline and experiment. The black West Indian comes from easy going islands. But his freedom is different. He finds this out in so many ways when he gets here.

I have told of my first visit home and the conflicts on my mind then. On my second visit about ten years later I had no personal tragedy to return to and had a longer chance to see Jamaica again. I was there for a month and was able to be with my family in normal circumstances. Yet again I could not tell them about my life in England. I still had to decide what to tell and what to suppress. They were still only interested in my successes, in the English people, how they dressed, how they lived, and the historic buildings. I didn't feel either happy or sad about England this time. I thought I would be happy to be out of England after so much rejection, I would be among my own people, the same as everyone else, no longer a stranger. Yet I found I was also missing England! I knew all along that I would be coming back to a life where I had to act a little sometimes for the sake of survival. It was difficult to feel real in England or in Jamaica. The visit was temporary so the adjustment needed only to be temporary too; the greater adjustment still had to take place in England.

It was not easy to settle in Jamaica. I found how wrong had been my belief that it would be easy to return. So many things were different, the way of speaking, the latest slang, the songs, the dress, the customs were different. I was a stranger in my own land of origin. I did not know where I belonged. I did not know what they wanted from me. I tried to be with them, one of them, to enjoy the things they enjoyed, though much of it was new to me and difficult to follow. In England I had the same problems. I also had to remain true to myself. I was happy to be in Jamaica because it was home, but the conflicts within me were the greater. I was not sure where my loyalty belonged. Was I to be loyal to my own people and tell them about my difficulties in England? Or was I to be loyal to the English and not let them down in the eyes of my own people? I returned to

England homesick for the Jamaican sun yet strangely pleased to be back, and life went on as before.

On my third visit a year or so later, it was much easier. The conflict about what to tell my people had gone. They had seen me three times now and they believed they knew all about England. I was just one of the family on another visit home. I had come to terms with the divided loyalty because I no longer felt threatened and trampled on in England. I had been through so much that I was sure I could deal with whatever the future had in store. I could see Jamaica more clearly. I toured the whole island, revisited all the childhood places and many others I did not know so well. I was at home. I did not feel homesick for England. I belonged, and for the first time I knew I belonged, among my own people in my own land. Yet because I belonged I knew I could also return to England and carry on in the ways I felt were best to help make sure of survival.

The years had slipped by and left their marks. Every so often I had met good people who stood by me and trusted me and who gave me back my ease and confidence. When one is suffering and the need is great the good people seem even better. One family I know in a village in Warwickshire enriched a significant period of my life in England. I always call on them if I am passing by. Knowing them makes that beautiful county even more beautiful. They make me feel there is nothing to fear anywhere. This family in the very heart of England reinstate in me the greatness of England that I had always heard about in my childhood. They are God's people, human and free.

I know my present feeling of confidence could be upset quite easily as it was when a politician made his first speech against coloured immigrants. Strange that it should be the very man who was my ultimate boss for so many years when thousands of other black immigrants were coming here to be doctors and nurses. His speech upset me because it came at a time when I believed people were coming to terms with black immigrants. He shattered the work I felt I had done by putting fears into the minds of the very people who had come to trust me. I was disappointed in the position he had taken. I was disappointed because of his influence. I was disappointed because he was an Englishman. I was disappointed because he let down so many good people. It told me that my confidence was not as justified as it had seemed. But it gave me a new challenge. I shall feel my confidence is more justified when speeches like his no longer perturb me.

My philosophy says go forward believing the best is yet to come. We must succeed because there is nothing else we can do. We cannot be anything but what we are, black people, but we are going to go on living, and part of living is trial and failure and more trial. There is no fear in the future for us if we go on trying. But if we allow pressures to push us back, we may behave more destructively. There is no fear in the future for white people who tackle the difficulties and walk ahead together with black people.

I have no fear and no anger in me now. But controlling them has taken time and effort. I thought perhaps that my story might serve to help white people, who are still fearful, to understand the experiences of black people and to see that there is a good chance for us all to live contentedly.

At the same time I want black people to feel that there is something for them here, but achieving it depends on their efforts. They will not be abused forever; they will find people who will accept them as equal. They did not come here to take over the country, or even a town, a district, a street or a house. They came here to help themselves and their families and in so doing to help this country as well. They came here because they were free, they wanted to remain free, to be respected. They only asked and expected to be respected also.

Eighteen

I Look Back

As the years progressed into the fifties, I recall the influx of black people into this country, from many Caribbean islands, but in particular Jamaica.

I noticed the reactions of my white friends. At first they showed astonishment, then they began to ask questions. Why are they coming? Why did they leave their beautiful islands? I too began to worry, but my worry was that the large number of black people could halt the progress that had been made. I was aware that I was living in a society rampant with institutionalised racism, and because this was a way of life it would be difficult to eradicate it. My fear was that sooner or later my black friends from overseas would encounter racism. I never wrote to Jamaica and my family to invite them to come here. I would never do so. I did not feel ashamed about that. I did not want them to experience what I had been through. I did not write to tell them about the situation in England, I just wrote enough to indicate my unhappiness at being away from home. During those years in the fifties I was very anxious that the newly arrived black people would also be rejected. Would they have the same difficulty finding rooms that I had had?

I made one or two black friends but not many. My problem was how to hold on to my white friends while developing friendships with black people. I found that I had been in England so long that I had begun to learn many white ways. It was now a question of re-learning Jamaican ways. I had accepted a model of race that had been handed down to me. Now I had to undo it.

I had accepted assimilation and had began to do the things that white people expected of me, e.g. talk like a white, even sometimes laugh at jokes about black people. Wherever I went the message from white people was 'be like us!' As I went along, I realised that as a black person, I could not assimilate into this society in that way. Instead I chose to be like myself.

I accept now the anti-racist model as the only model for Afro-Caribbean and British black people. My belief in this was strengthened as I took up training in racism awareness. The anti-racism model allows for black and white people working together, sharing together, being in charge of each other. It is full of conflicts, but I believe that it is the only model that will enable black people to feel free in this society. Accept me as I am!

I learned about British racism and how it began. The explorers who went to Africa and returned to give British people misleading reports about black people. This was the beginning of the slave trade, which involved some 15 million black people being taken from Africa to the western hemisphere for economic reasons. A third of these died on route.

I felt better informed. I found out who I was, and where I came from. This, I feel, strengthened my will to work and support people who were victims of racism. It also enabled me to run courses and train people in anti-racism practice.

I regard a racist society as a society in which the people are inheritors of the legacy of racism, which is passed on from generation to generation. Society seems to question less and less as racism becomes institutionalised. It is important that white people take this issue on board. We need to work together to conquer racism. We have to prevent black youth from being alienated, in effect denied education and forced into creating its own sub-cultures, which further enhance the alienation process. The worrying thing about this is that the majority of people think that all black youth belongs to this sub-culture. I believe that this form of stereotyping of black youth is not helpful for race relations.

I am also concerned about the effect of racism on younger black children, who are in school suffering from these effects. I recall visiting a black friend when his nine year old came home from school and said: 'Daddy, why wasn't I born white? I don't want to be black', and started to cry. I see this as the beginning of self hate, to hate one's own colour. I have no doubt that many young black people in the sub-culture have also developed self hate. For a black person, racism is twenty-four hours a day, there is no let up. Despite the difficulties I have experienced during my journey in this country, I did survive. It was not easy, but there has been some change. It is much easier for me to live in this society than it was in the early years. Race Relations legislation has been enforced. Racism is being talked about openly. Black and white seem to be mixing more, but in reality racism has not lessened to any great degree.

I believe that it would be in the interest of better race relations if young children at school were made properly aware of the concept of racism and its consequences.

As racism has been institutionalised, white people may not always be aware of their racist projections, so therefore black people have a role to play in helping their white friends to realise that their behaviour may be racist. Not to accuse them, but to draw their attention to their behaviour. Greater interaction between black and white is essential.

I believe in the process of dialogue which I believe is the only way for black and white people to work together, challenge racism, and find a way forward.

December, 1949

At a wedding in Holland, 1952

On the boat to Trinidad and Jamaica, 1957 (Eric, bottom right)

Venezuela, 1958

Banstead, 1959

Manchester, 1962

Viney Green Children's Home, Bristol, 1968

Christmas 1968

With fellow students in Bristol, 1969

In the office, 1970

Eric Ferron, 1994